M000035767

STAND WITH CHRIST

WHY MISSIONARIES CAN'T SIGN THE
2000 BAPTIST FAITH AND MESSAGE

EDITED BY

ROBERT O'BRIEN

SMYTH&HELWYS
PUBLISHING, INCORPORATED · MACON, GEORGIA

Smyth & Helwys Publishing, Inc.
6316 Peake Road
Macon, Georgia 31210-3960
1-800-747-3016
©2002 by Smyth & Helwys Publishing
All rights reserved.
Printed in the United States of America.

The views and opinions expressed in this book do not necessarily
represent those of Smyth & Helwys Publishing.

The paper used in this publication meets the min-
imum requirements of American National
Standard for Information Sciences—Permanence
of Paper for Printed Library Materials.
ANSI Z39.48–1984. (alk. paper)

Library of Congress Cataloging-in-Publication Data

O'Brien, Robert, 1939-
    Stand with Christ : why missionaries can't sign the 2000 Baptist faith
and message / by Robert O'Brien.
        p. cm.
    ISBN 1-57312-403-6 (alk. paper)
1. Baptist faith and message. 2. Southern Baptist Convention—Creeds.
3. Southern Baptist Convention. International Mission Board. 4.
Missionaries—Religious life. I. Title.
    BX6462.7 O25 2002
    238'.6132—dc21

                                                        2002007727

TABLE OF CONTENTS

FOREWORD

BY WALTER B. SHURDEN

This is a book *by* Baptists. Most Baptists, especially Baptists of the South, will readily recognize the writers—Russell Dilday, Keith Parks, James Dunn, Catherine Allen, Charles Wade, David Currie, Charles Deweese, John Pierce, Kenneth Massey, Bruce Prescott, Earl Martin, and editor Robert O'Brien. Marinated in the Baptist tradition of a free and responsible conscience, each of these writers carries a sterling Baptist portfolio. They deserve to be heard. They should be heeded.

This is also a book *about* Baptists. Specifically, it is a book about the Southern Baptist Convention and its deliberate, but unbaptistic, move toward creedalism. Inherent in this embrace of creedalism has been a theological and organizational hardwiring of the denomination. The Southern Baptist Church, an unbaptistic animal that W. W. Barnes warned of in a prophetic book of 1934,[1] emerges out of the shadows of Baptist congregationalism, even amid much talk of the autonomy of the local church. This theological hardwiring, as Russell Dilday notes in his chapter, has a note of strict Calvinism in it, unfamiliar to most Southern Baptists. In the face of the theological creedalism and the organizational centralization, the writers of these chapters call for freedom of conscience for all Baptists, but especially for SBC missionaries.

Three *"C"* words dominate this book: *Creedalism, Centralization, Conscience.* The message of this book is about denominational centralization. It is about conscience, especially freedom of conscience, an historic Baptist principle, as it struggles in the face of both creedalism and centralization. The primary concern of the writers of this book, however, is the first *"C"* word: *creedalism.* Anyone who denies that the Southern Baptist Convention has evolved from an anti-confessional to a pro-creedal denomination either does not know or intentionally distorts Southern Baptist history. Here are the six stages of the evolution of creedalism within the Southern Baptist Convention (SBC).

Stage one: The SBC opposed the adoption of a confession of faith of any and every kind. When the founders of the SBC met in Augusta, Georgia, in 1845 to form the SBC, they deliberately refused to adopt *any* previous Baptist confession of faith. It is true that Baptists before them had adopted such doctrinal statements. It is also true that groups of Southern Baptist people, such as associations and institutions, adopted confessional statements during the nineteenth century. However, the SBC intentionally rejected not only creeds but also confessions of faith in 1845. "We have constructed for our basis no new creed; acting in this matter upon a Baptist aversion for all creeds but the Bible."[2]

In 1846, only one year after the SBC was organized, William B. Johnson, the first president of the SBC, wrote a little book that few Southern Baptists have ever heard of. He called it *The Gospel Developed through the Government and Order of the Churches of Jesus Christ.* One of Johnson's major arguments in his book is that a local Baptist church is a Christocracy. A church is a body of believers ruled by Christ.

Because Baptist churches are Christocracies, Johnson argued that Baptists do not need confessions of faith. Please read, slowly and carefully, the following words of one of the most prominent Southern Baptists at the formation of the SBC:

> Keeping this first principle in view, that Christ is the *one* Lord of his people, and has given the revelation of his will in a complete and perfect code of laws and precepts, the impropriety of having any human selection and compilation of these, as a *standard of faith and practice,* is manifestly evident. If it be said that the compilation thus prepared contains what is in the Bible, the question comes up, why then form the compilation? Why not use *The Bible as the standard?* Can man present God's system in a selection and compilation of some of its parts, better than God has himself done it, as a whole in his own book?[3]

Johnson, this first president and founder of the SBC, was pro-biblical and very committed to the truth claims of Scripture, but he was thoroughly anti-creedal, even anti-confessional.

While anti-confessional, William B. Johnson was ardently Christ-centered. Unity in Baptist life, he contended, came not from confessions of faith or imposed doctrinal statements. Unity came from each believer being conformed to the will of Christ. Southern Baptist fundamentalists today would berate his approach by calling it "theological minimalism." Dismissing it with such derogatory language, however, does not abolish the fact that Johnson was Christ-centered rather than creed-centered. Hear Johnson again:

> The value of the Christocratic form of government consists in this, that each acting in reference to Christ alone, all will be conformed to Christ, and thus conformed to each other. And this is the manner by which uniformity is to be secured and preserved, and not by confederations of churches, confessions of

faith, or written codes of formularies framed by man, as bonds of union for the churches of Christ.[4]

From 1845 to 1925, the SBC lived comfortably without any doctrinal statement.

Stage Two: Southern Baptist fundamentalists issue calls for strict and rigid orthodoxy. This happened first in the 1920s, again in the 1960s, and again beginning in 1979 and lasting to the present.

Stage Three: Fundamentalists, contrary to the SBC heritage, issue a call for a doctrinal statement to guard the orthodoxy. Prominent Southern Baptists resisted this call, thinking it unwise, but SBC leadership, in an effort to pacify fundamentalists, acquiesced to the adoption of *A Statement of the Baptist Faith and Message* in 1925 (*BFM25*). However, the SBC carefully designated the *BFM* as *descriptive* and *not prescriptive*. Southern Baptists of the 1920s did not force compliance with the *BFM25*.

W. W. Barnes, professor of church history at Southwestern Baptist Theological Seminary for forty years (1913–1953), warned Southern Baptists in 1934 of the consequences of adopting the *BFM25*. Calling the statement a "creed," Barnes said:

> The doctrinal effort did result in the adoption, by the Convention, of what amounts to a creedal statement—*the first time the Southern Baptist Convention ever considered doing such a thing.* Strange to say, the controversy that raged in the convention was not over the question whether the convention was, or ought to be, a creed-making body, but the question was: What should be included in the creed to be adopted? The reception that that creed has received, or perhaps one should say, has not received, seems to suggest that Southern Baptists are not yet ready for doctrinal centralization, but the first step has been taken. It may be another century, but if and when the doctrinal question again arises, succeeding generations can point to 1925 and say that the Southern Baptist Convention, having once adopted a creed, can do so again. Perhaps by that time other centralizing forces will have been developed and the convention may have the means and the method of compelling congregations to take notice of the creed then adopted.[5]

Barnes's timing was off! It did not take another century, only seventy-five years.

Stage Four: Fundamentalists spearhead revisions to the creed to guarantee the orthodoxy. The SBC revised the *BFM* in 1963 (*BFM63*), 1998 (*BFM98*), and 2000 (*BFM2000*).

Stage Five: Fundamentalists call for the imposition of the revised creed on individual Baptists to make binding the orthodoxy. Here is where this book comes in. It is a ringing Baptist protest of the changed nature and the imposition of *BFM2000* upon Baptist individuals, especially missionaries.[6]

Stage Six: Fundamentalists camouflage their creedalism with rhetoric regarding the SBC's historic anti-creedal posture. In other words, they denounce with history what they practice in the present.[7]

My hope is that this book will be read and discussed by Baptists of all theological stripes. I especially hope that young people in our Baptist churches, often gripped by a pack mentality, may have the chance to study and benefit from what these faithful Baptists have written. The professor in me will not permit me to close without giving additional bibliography. If you are intrigued by what you read here, let me encourage you to secure a copy of W. W. Barnes's 1934 book, *The Southern Baptist Convention: A Study in the Development of Ecclesiology.* Only eighty pages long, it is a masterful, in some ways a tragic, piece of prophecy of what has happened to the SBC. Barnes's book can be read easily and quickly. If, however, you are ready to put your intellectual and spiritual boots on for some rigorous work, read carefully *Against Returning to Egypt: Exposing and Resisting Credalism in the Southern Baptist Convention* by Jeff Pool.

NOTES

[1] William Wright Barnes, *The Southern Baptist Convention: A Study in The Development of Ecclesiology* (Seminary Hill TX: Published by the author, 1934).

[2] *Annual, SBC, 1845*, p. 19.

[3] William B. Johnson, *The Gospel Developed through the Government and Order of the Churches of Jesus Christ* (Richmond: H. K. Ellyson, 1846), 197.

[4] Ibid., 200.

[5] Barnes, 59-60. Italics are mine and for emphasis.

[6] Jeff Pool, *Against Returning to Egypt: Exposing and Resisting Credalism in the Southern Baptist Convention* (Macon GA: Mercer University Press, 1998), argues convincingly that the adoption of the *Report of the Presidential Theological Study Commission* in 1994 by the SBC marked "the official inauguration" of creedalism in the SBC. I agree with W. W. Barnes that the process began in 1925, but I acknowledge the truth of Pool's argument regarding more recent SBC creedalism.

[7] Pool makes this same point regarding the *Report of the Presidential Theological Study Commission.* See ibid., 5.

INTRODUCTION:
A DIFFERENT "HILL TO DIE ON"

BY ROBERT O'BRIEN

Its leaders call it a "Battle for the Bible." They extol it as a "hill to die on." It (the takeover by fundamentalists of the Southern Baptist Convention) has consumed, at this writing, twenty-three years of the life and ministry of Southern Baptists. It has fired, intimidated, misrepresented, and discredited those who oppose it, disagree with it, or interpret things differently. Some of its "soldiers" have even boasted that honors and promotions have come to those who have figurative "blood on their hands" in its cause.

And its end is not in sight. The takeover has moved from consuming the SBC structure into a campaign to control Baptist churches, associations, state conventions, and institutions. It seeks to occupy every nook and cranny of Southern Baptist life and spread its influence around the world.

As you read this, it is splitting churches and associations—and has already ruptured at least three state Baptist conventions into competing bodies. It has launched a full-court press to make its new field manual, the 2000 *Baptist Faith and Message (BFM2000)*, mandatory in Baptist churches, associations, state conventions, and institutions.

BFM2000 has already become mandatory—in its every jot and tittle—for all SBC seminary professors, agency employees, and missionaries on the world's far-flung mission fields. It seeks to turn them into theological clones.

Ironically, the hot-hearted protest of earlier years of the takeover had subsided to a large degree. It would likely have remained that way except for a series of top-down mandates in early 2002 that sent a chill through Baptists. Previously, many of them actually had been oblivious to what was really happening.

In what seemed like a frantic rush to gain total control, the series of four mandates that changed the mood of Baptists came out from three SBC entities:

- The International Mission Board called on all missionaries to sign an affirmation of *BFM2000*, despite promises by IMB President Jerry Rankin that it would not happen on his watch.
- The North American Mission Board refused to continue endorsing ordained women for the chaplaincy. (NAMB later also asked North American-based missionaries to sign *BFM2000*.)
- NAMB threatened to seize control of the autonomous District of Columbia Baptist Convention, as John Pierce points out in a chapter in this book. Later, it defunded the D.C. Convention when it refused to comply.
- The Executive Committee refused to take funds from a new moderate state convention that split in 2002 from the fundamentalist-controlled convention in Missouri. The Executive Committee recognizes new breakaway fundamentalist state conventions in Texas and Virginia.

Henry Green, a Baptist pastor in Annapolis, Maryland, wrote an open letter calling the mandates "four smoking gun" issues among Southern Baptists. They kick-started a backlash that has whipped across the Baptist landscape, especially in Texas, where Baptists took a firm stand to help missionaries whose integrity will not allow them to sign *BFM2000*.

The backlash also resulted in Smyth & Helwys Publishing and its editors Mark McElroy and Keith Gammons commissioning this book to take a serious look at how dominating creedalism has spawned a downward spiral of freedom in the SBC—especially focusing on why missionaries and others cannot sign *BFM2000*.

Letters to missionaries from Jerry Rankin, urging them to sign total allegiance to *BFM2000*, created the most intense backlash. Otherwise, the furor might have faded. As veteran missionary and missions professor Earl Martin says in a chapter in this book, "It opened the eyes of many Baptists who had naively rationalized that the political strife of two decades of takeover of the SBC by fundamentalists would somehow leave their missionaries untouched."

A variety of seasoned and qualified Baptist observers spent hours of their time to research and write their perspectives on alarming developments that could poison the Baptist atmosphere around the world. They come from the fields of Baptist history, theology, missions, pastoral and denominational leadership, journalism, and ethics. They express themselves with passion and conviction.

No one expects every reader to agree with everything these writers say. At points, they would differ from each other. Even the editor of this book would not have said some things exactly the way some writers said them.

But that's the point of it all. Baptists have a heritage of freedom to agree to disagree about certain things, while getting on with the "main thing"—the gospel and ministry of Jesus Christ. The SBC takeover has systematically endeavored to eliminate the "wiggle room" for that freedom, as one SBC leader openly admitted.

That's the problem with *BFM2000*.

No Baptist who thinks about it seriously would deny that the framers of *BFM2000* have every right to believe every word of what they have written and certainly have every right to sign it as their own belief. The problem comes, as the writers in this book attest, when a power structure turns a general confession of faith into a creedal, self-described "instrument of doctrinal accountability" to which all must pledge total and absolute allegiance. When a confession of faith that someone could sign willingly becomes a statement that others must sign, willing or not, it becomes an enforced creed that tramples on soul freedom and the priesthood of the believer.

My maternal grandmother, a stern but loving Baptist preacher's widow, had a saying when chastising me for overstepping my bounds: "Your rights end where mine begin." That bugged me then, but it has lived on in my heart as a jewel of wisdom.

If I foolishly denied that Jesus Christ is the Son of God, my fellow Baptists would have every right to chastise me—even suggest that I don't belong in Baptist ministry. The inspired written word of God could not be clearer about that and a variety of other things that are basic fundamentals of the faith (not to be confused with *fundamentalism* or *fundamentalist*).

But all Scripture isn't that clear. Honest differences of interpretation exist, but *BFM2000* won't permit that—especially in certain areas, where *BFM2000* enshrines certain interpretations as absolute and leaves no room for healthy discussion about them or disagreement with them.

- It enshrines the interpretation that Jesus Christ is bound inside the pages of Scripture rather than standing above all things. It removes him as the criterion through which we interpret Scripture. My grandmother had another saying: "Run like a scalded dog when anyone puts Jesus in anything other than first place." I didn't understand that then, but I do now, and it now lives on in my heart as my "Scalded Dog Notion of Christology." There's Scripture to back that up—although not available in *BFM2000*. Read what Russell Dilday, Bruce Prescott, Earl Martin, and others have to say about the role of Jesus Christ.
- It enshrines one interpretation of the role of women in marriage and ministry, despite any other evidence that can be cited from Scripture and the guidance of the Holy Spirit. Read insights offered by Catherine Allen and the other chapter authors.

- It enshrines itself as a creed, flying in the face of Baptist history and heritage, stifling soul liberty, and becoming an enforcer rather than an enabler of faith. Charles Deweese and James Dunn make that clear in their chapters.
- It enshrines a transformation of individual priesthood of the believer into a corporate priesthood of the believer and other things that authors in this book explore.

This approach characterizes fundamentalists, who go beyond the basic fundamentals of the faith to embrace legalistic mindset that codifies rigid regulations and interpretations, demands absolute doctrinal conformity, and tolerates no dissent.

Many Baptists believe that what the fundamentalists began as a so-called "Battle for the Bible" has become a reverse campaign to prevent them from imposing a man-made prism (*BFM2000*) that shrinks the Bible into something less than itself. They also believe that removing Jesus Christ from the *Baptist Faith and Message* as the criterion for interpretation of Scripture shrinks him from Lord of all things into something resembling a tribal deity.

For many years, the generals and soldiers of the takeover clubbed other Baptists over the head with the word "inerrancy"—but, ironically, that word does not appear in *BFM2000*. That led Dr. Dilday to make this observation in his chapter:

> The omission does seem curious, since so much of the twenty-year controversy centered on enforcing the use of the term "inerrant" to describe the nature of the Bible. Does that mean the term is no longer deemed necessary? Was it a real issue all those years, or just a semantic difference used as a "smoke screen" for a power grab, as many believe?

Now, the emphasis is on a manmade creed that enshrines certain interpretations as absolute, and it's certainly not "inerrant" because it overlooks "troublesome" Scripture to the contrary.

Kenneth Massey makes an eloquent point in his chapter:

> Whenever we lock up our beliefs (right or wrong) in a rigid system of manmade propositions, we hinder the Spirit from moving and stretching us to deeper truth. Does this mean there is no absolute truth? I say "No!" It means there is no absolute human understanding. It means human interpretation is always incomplete. It means we never live up to or completely understand divine absolutes. I think the authors and promoters of *BFM2000* believe they are protecting the faith and preserving sound doctrine. I share many of their concerns about theological entropy. Creating an inflexible wineskin of denominational accountability, however, is not the solution. No confession or creed will ever hold the new wine of God's Spirit.

What's the true "hill to die on"? Is it the SBC takeover, as one prominent takeover architect describes it, or is it freedom in Jesus Christ? Many Baptists have risen up to say the latter. What's more important for Baptists? Is it figuratively to spill the blood of fellow believers in doctrinal combat, or is to spread the message of the blood that Jesus Christ literally spilled to bring salvation? Many Baptists have risen up to say the latter.

Shirley, my wife, also has a saying when I get too overbearing. "Enough is enough and too much is too much." That bugs me when I hear it, but it lives on in my heart as a jewel of wisdom. That's what the writers in this book are saying in different ways with strong conviction. Enough is enough. Too much is too much. And here's why. Like David Currie, one of the chapter authors, these writers have drawn a "line on the ground." As general editor of this book, I appreciate their hard work and insightful writing and the fact that two prominent Baptists—historian Walter Shurden and foreign missions veteran Keith Parks—agreed to add their insights in the foreword and the afterword.

Many Baptists today can remember nothing but the controversy. I began writing about Southern Baptists thirty-seven years ago and have done so across the U. S. and at least fifty foreign countries. I remember when Southern Baptists, cooperating across a diverse spectrum, reached the zenith of their missions endeavor. They coexisted in an "emulsion" of trust and mutual respect and their influence spread to all fifty states and to many nations around the world.

Southern Baptists even pursued an idealistic, but noble, goal in their earlier Bold Mission Thrust effort to reach the world for Christ by the year 2000. Other Christians set similar goals. Realistically speaking, it was not to be—and missiologists began adding the phrase "2000 and Beyond" to their goals. But it generated a lot of emphasis on the "main thing"—the gospel and ministry of Jesus.

SBC "takeover politics," and its attendant strategies, however, certainly detracted from the spirit of that goal for Southern Baptists. Doctrinal control overshadowed missions. Takeover politics, continuing unrelentingly today into every corner of Baptist life, dissolved that trust and broke down that "emulsion" and sent Baptists into a dizzying swirl of divisiveness and separation.

In some ways, it resembles a modern-day *Diaspora,* with new Baptist seminaries, churches, networks, and ministries spreading across the nation and the world as a result. The new *Diaspora* has birthed Christian entrepreneurs with new concern for evangelism, missions, church growth, Christian ethics, theological education, publishing, dissemination of legitimate news, and preservation of Baptist history and heritage. All that has come to life through at least a dozen new seminaries, the Cooperative Baptist Fellowship, the Baptist Center for Ethics, the Mainstream Baptist Network, Smyth & Helwys Publishing, Associated Baptist Press, and *Baptists Today.*

The Word of God has refused to be chained. So why should we care what the SBC does? Why not just go about our business? Well, we *should* go about our business, but we *also* should care about anything that hurts and misleads people.

We should care because of the havoc that creedalism and top-down control can unleash on the world's missions fields. Read what Earl Martin has to say about that in two thoughtful chapters in this book.

We should care because thousands of Baptists in churches across the U. S. have not understood what is really happening. They didn't realize—or are just learning—that a battle once remote in their busy lives now inhabits their churches and conventions.

Pastors say, "We never thought it would come to this." A layman says, "I didn't even realize there was a controversy until 1995." A Sunday school class, exposed to it in dialogue in 2002, sits dumbfounded. A congregation, finally hearing about it from the pulpit in 2002, goes slack-jawed. Others have thought it was just a "preacher fight" of no consequence to them. Many, now growing up into leaders, were children or weren't even born when all of this began. The lessons of history have bypassed them. The list goes on.

Calling these people ignorant or unworthy of concern "after all these years" sadly oversimplifies the truth. Many denominational and church "gatekeepers"—pastors, editors, teachers, and others—have shielded them from direct observation of it because they fear they can't handle controversy, they might learn too much of the truth, or it will hurt their giving. Or they rationalize it as "the Christian thing to do," or they just want to "lie low" and hope it will go away.

But what about the question of getting on with the main business at hand? That's the long-range hope for all who want to minister in the name of Jesus Christ and many have already stepped in that direction.

Hope burgeons in such states as Texas and Virginia, where Baptists have risen up to say they will cooperate with the SBC but not to the exclusion of diverse Baptists and not at the price of lock-step conformity. Texas Baptists reach out to churches and communities through their "Building Relationships: 2002" initiative and have launched a transition fund to help missionaries who refuse to sign *BFM2000* and also a Chaplaincy Endorsement Board open to all qualified men and women.

Charles Wade, executive director of the Baptist General Convention of Texas, says in his chapter: "Some will say that we are distancing ourselves from Southern Baptists. Let me say again, as I have said before, we stand ready to work with Southern Baptists. We have not wanted the things that have happened . . . to happen. We are focused on a lost world that needs our Savior and his gospel. Why these distractions? Why these extra requirements?"

Another example of hope was rising—fresh and new—in Virginia as this book went to press. It's reported in some detail here because of the widespread interest it has generated from Baptists around the country as a possible model for unity.

The object of hope centers on a vision called "Kingdom Advance" by John Upton, a former Southern Baptist missionary to Taiwan and new executive director of the Baptist General Association of Virginia (BGAV). Kingdom Advance did not originate as a response to controversy but as a way to expand and magnify missions and evangelism at a time when the state population growth outstrips Christian growth, when there is a growing crisis in church leadership development, and when ministries are opening up all around the world. But a special called meeting of the BGAV on May 10, 2002, voted overwhelmingly to endorse Kingdom Advance as way for diverse Baptists to work together. Excitement permeated the state and reverberated back from observers in other states. People waited eagerly as Upton and four "design teams" formulated the final Kingdom Advance structure to take to the BGAV's annual meeting in November 2002 for a final vote.

Kingdom Advance envisions the BGAV and its Virginia Baptist Mission Board (VBMB) as an umbrella under which diverse Baptists may cooperate on the "main thing"— spreading the gospel and ministry of Jesus Christ while maintaining their church autonomy and freedom to choose. Could this approach recreate the trust and mutual respect that will put diverse Virginia Baptists, and those who choose to partner with them, back into that creative "emulsion" that benefited Southern Baptists for so many years? Time will tell.

Kingdom Advance envisions churches finding open avenues to Virginia Baptist ministries around the state, nation, and globe, while maintaining their diversity. It envisions aggressively starting new churches in Virginia and rejuvenating existing ones, identifying and developing a new generation of men and women as leaders for Virginia Baptist congregations and ministries, and empowering pastors and other church leaders to carry out their ministries more effectively.

Kingdom Advance could open up wider missions options for all BGAV churches to find "a place at the table," regardless of what Baptist missions efforts they choose to support. It envisions a flexible approach to missions that would avoid competing with other Baptist bodies, such as the SBC's International and North American Mission Boards, the Cooperative Baptist Fellowship, or the Baptist World Alliance. Instead, it would expand current cooperation with these and other entities and open opportunities for Virginia Baptists to partner with other Baptists around the world.

"BGAV local churches will decide, in the Baptist way, what they will support. We will offer options and opportunities to all of them who wish to participate," Upton said.

Upton said his vision "bubbled up" from the grassroots as he traveled the state to glean input from over five hundred pastors and a variety of other Baptists from the top leadership to the pew. He heard three consistent questions: (1) Can you give us something bigger than us to excite our church? (2) Is there a place for us at the denominational table? (3) Is there any way to lift ourselves out of this denominational controversy and get on with the gospel and ministry of Jesus Christ?

"Kingdom Advance says, 'Yes' to all three questions," Upton said.

But a messenger to the special called meeting in May 2002 strongly disagreed on the grounds that it was too inclusive of diverse Baptists. He characterized the day of the called meeting as "a sad day" that history books would record as one of "Kingdom Divided," not one of "Kingdom Advance."

Upton answered with one sentence that drew a standing ovation from messengers and visitors in the large sanctuary of First Baptist Church in Charlottesville, Virginia—the church where Southern Baptist missions pioneer Lottie Moon was baptized in 1858.

"It's my prayer that they [the history books] will record that today Baptists divided became Baptists united," Upton replied.

Upton also quickly affirmed the response of another messenger, who rose to say that he supported Kingdom Advance but hoped that Virginia Baptists would always allow a dissenting voice to be heard. That, Upton said later, has been the point all along—and certainly a point that too many people have missed in the long Southern Baptist struggle.

"We all may disagree about some things," Upton said, "but we are going to find things we can agree on and get on with the main thing—the gospel and ministry of Jesus Christ."

A LINE ON THE GROUND

BY DAVID R. CURRIE

People will long remember the contribution that John Leland of Virginia made to religious liberty. Virginia, a state hailed as the cradle of religious liberty in America, still stands strong as an island of independence and freedom. Most Virginia Baptists know what it means to be Baptist.

So do many other Baptists, including my fellow, freedom-loving Texans, who have stood up during the crisis in the Southern Baptist Convention to say "enough is enough." Many Baptists from a number of states, in fact, have drawn a line on the ground. History has many examples of that kind of line.

A South Carolinian named William Barrett Travis, legend says, drew a line on the ground inside the Alamo in Texas in early March 1836. Only thirty-two people had responded to four calls for reinforcements for the embattled Alamo. The situation seemed hopeless for the remaining defenders. So Travis drew the line and said, "Those of you who will stay and fight until the end, step across this line."

History tells us all the men but one crossed the line, knowing that step was a step that would end in death. Those who stepped across came from Virginia, Arkansas, Alabama, Mississippi, North Carolina, South Carolina, Louisiana, Georgia, Pennsylvania, Kentucky, Missouri, Ohio, Illinois, Maryland, Rhode Island, New York, Tennessee, England, Ireland, and Germany.

Why did a group of such diverse people do that? *Freedom!* Not the eternal freedom Baptists have been contending for over the past two decades, but another kind of important freedom—political freedom, freedom to dream and to live their lives. Today, Baptists from many places have realized they must step across a line—no matter what the repercussions—to defend *freedom in Christ.*

Some twenty-three years after the Southern Baptist Convention (SBC) battle began, the SBC International Mission Board (IMB) has drawn another line on the ground. But it's a different kind of line. The IMB has finally succumbed to what every other SBC agency has done by saying to the missionaries, in effect, "If you will give up your freedom, step over this line and sign the 2000 *Baptist Faith and Message*."

Many believe it really means: "If you will replace Jesus Christ as Lord with the SBC as lord, step over this line."

Significant words describe the battle we are in today—a battle as old as the first century: "For the law was given through Moses, but grace and truth came through Jesus Christ" (John 1:17). The battle revolves around these two questions: (1) Is Jesus about law? or (2) Is Jesus about grace and truth?

The answers to those questions also address questions about traditional Baptist men and women, who have coalesced from across the US to resist the legalistic inroads of fundamentalism. Why do we resist fundamentalism? Why do we try to preserve the Baptist witness in the US and around the world? Why not just "go along to get along"? Many Baptists have done that. Since traditional Baptists and fundamentalist Baptists both believe in Jesus, why can't we work it out, reconcile, and focus on the "main thing"—Jesus Christ? Why do traditional Baptists do what they do?

WHY DO TRADITIONAL BAPTISTS DO WHAT THEY DO?

. . . Because of Jesus.

I believe in this "Jesus stuff," as I like to call it. Recently, I preached the funeral of one of my best friends, and it was my faith in Jesus that gave me the strength to preach. I believe Jesus is the way to salvation. I believe Jesus was God in the flesh, fully human and fully divine.

The Jesus preached by many fundamentalists resembles the character of God preached by some of the religious leaders of Jesus' day. They saw a God who was narrow, petty, legalistic, judgmental, and more interested in the surface details of the law than in its spiritual intentionality. Some religious leaders of that day focused more on being "technically right" than on being morally right. They opposed a compassionate interpretation of the law. Thus, they criticized Jesus when he healed on the Sabbath (technically the wrong day), talked to women in public (technically the wrong sex), or traveled through Samaria (technically populated by the wrong race).

Many modern fundamentalists also preach a Jesus who is judgmental, angry, and mean-spirited. For them, what's good is less important than what's legal. For them, the law determines the truth, not grace. William Barclay says in his commentary on Galatians: "What Paul is saying is, this legalistic movement may not have gone very far yet, but you must root it out before it destroys your whole religion."[1] This sort of fundamentalism will destroy the Baptist witness in America and in other cultures where our missionaries work. We must stop it from doing that.

Division in Southern Baptist life results, most of all, from our belief in a "different" Jesus! Traditional Baptists and fundamentalist Baptists have different, irreconcilable visions of the gospel of Jesus Christ. The Jesus of the Scriptures is a person of love, compassion, and grace. The danger of rigid fundamentalism is portraying Jesus as a legalistic literalist.

The Jesus written about in the Scriptures was severely criticized by the fundamentalist religious leaders of his day. Likewise, traditional Baptists are severely criticized by the current fundamentalist leadership of the Southern Baptist Convention.

Jesus was, and traditional Baptists are, criticized for the same reason—their understanding of the character and nature of God. As traditional Baptists, we resist fundamentalism because it does not focus on the Jesus of grace and truth, only on surface elements of divine laws revealed to Moses.

Many fundamentalists are more interested in telling people how to live than telling people about the power to live—Jesus, the Christ. Fundamentalism fights a cultural war, while we fight a spiritual war.

In short, to borrow from Andrae Crouch, we believe Jesus is the answer for the world today. Above him is no other. The heart of Christianity is a personal relationship with Jesus. We must resist fundamentalism because America and the world need a Baptist witness focused on Jesus, not on power; focused on grace, not on a narrow interpretation of the law; and focused on compassion, not on judgment.

Baptists will reunite when Baptists hold up the Jesus of the Scriptures. We must become obsessed with Jesus, with preaching Jesus, with living for Jesus, with imitating Jesus, with telling people about Jesus, and with doing good deeds in Jesus' name and for his sake.

The result of the past two decades of conflict in Baptist life must be a revival of our focus on Jesus. We do what we do because Jesus deserves to be presented truthfully.

. . . Because we believe the Bible.

The myth of the past two decades is that Baptists are battling over whether or not to accept the authority of Scripture. This is now and has always been an outright lie!

Let me be clear about Scripture: I do not believe we have any knowledge of Jesus contradictory to the context of the Scriptures. I also believe we have a personal relationship with Jesus, the living Christ. He helps us interpret the Scriptures and interacts with us daily in a way consistent with the Scriptures. The Bible is our final authority in all matters of faith and practice. Jesus will never reveal himself inconsistently with the written Word.

Traditional Baptists believe the Bible. I don't know a single Baptist who does not believe the Bible is our final authority in matters of faith and practice. I don't know a single Baptist who does not base his or her personal beliefs on the Bible. I don't know any Baptists who believe that their personal beliefs are based on teachings that are "extra-biblical" in origination.

Problems come from human attempts to impose their own imperfect understandings on the Word. Many seem to forget, when it comes to interpreting Scripture, that Jesus is alive as the Holy Spirit. He reveals himself daily to us in many ways, but always consistent with his character as revealed in Scripture.

Jesus is the Living Word of God above *all* things. "All things were made through him, and without him was not anything made that was made" (John 1:3). He is not bound within the pages of Scripture but stands above all things, including Scripture.

We find God many ways. We can know him long before we know Scripture, through the Holy Spirit. He guides us as we read and interpret Scripture. Without Jesus, we cannot know the truth of Scripture, and we cannot interpret Scripture with integrity.

When the 2000 *Baptist Faith and Message* (*BFM2000*) statement deleted reference to Jesus Christ as the "criterion by which the Bible is to be interpreted," it sent shock waves through many Baptists in America and other countries. They saw it as the final insult in a series of events that fracture Baptist heritage and imperil freedom in Jesus Christ.

Biblical truth is eternal, and its application is constantly expanding, under the Lordship of the Living Word, to meet the needs of modern society—whether it's the first century, the eleventh century, or the twenty-first century. That's the beauty and power of God's eternal written word. Its authority transcends all time, and its application is relevant for any time. The Bible is a timeless book, and its truth is absolute! It was written for its own time and period, but its principles are eternal in application.

Fundamentalism is in danger of locking the Bible's truth in time and space, making the Bible irrelevant for modern problems and situations. We must rescue it for our generation and generations to come.

An example: I know of no Baptist church that has ordained a woman that did not do so based on its understanding of Bible teachings. I do not question Paul's writings about women being silent in the church, as he wrote to a first-century audience where they relegated women to non-equality. Paul gave the exact, perfect, God-inspired advice to churches he was writing to in the first century. His words were inspired and appropriate.

God also told Paul to write that "in Christ, there is no male or female, Jew or Gentile, free or slave" (Gal 3:29). This is the eternal principle of Paul's teaching. In Christ, all are equal. Both our sons and our "daughters shall prophesy" (Acts 2:7b).

Reading Paul's message to first-century Christians in the context of the culture in which he wrote is not "liberal." Interpreting his words differently in light of modern society also is not liberal. Failing to interpret Scripture in light of modern culture, under the Lordship of Jesus Christ, is to deny its eternal truths and make the Bible appear to be a dead book with no authority in our time.

I believe that women whom God calls should be ministers, deacons, or church leaders precisely because I believe in the authority of Scripture and the eternal principles taught in Scripture. I *do not* believe these things *in spite of* Scripture but *because of* Scripture! *BFM2000*, as you will read in other chapters, would lock in a much narrower interpretation of the role of women.

I respect those who disagree with me and do not question their commitment to the authority of Scripture. But I also believe that traditional Baptists must counteract legalistic interpretations of the Bible that have *locked its eternal truths in time*—and made them prescriptions for a time long past. We must preserve the authority of Scripture *for* modern society, not *from* modern society. The Bible's truths are eternal.

Traditional Baptists, more so than fundamentalists, have a high view of Scripture. We believe its principles have application in all situations and will continue to have application in the twenty-first century. The world needs the Bible and its testimony to the saving power of Jesus Christ. The world needs eternal, timeless, absolute truth, and we are seeking to preserve it.

That's why the 1963 *Baptist Faith and Message* statement's preamble says this:

> Baptists are people who profess a living faith. This faith is rooted and grounded in Jesus Christ, who is "the same yesterday, and today, and forever." Therefore, the sole authority for faith and practice among Baptists is Jesus Christ, whose will is revealed in the Holy Scriptures. A living faith must experience a growing understanding of truth and must be continually interpreted and related to the needs of each new generation.

The Southern Baptist Convention also created shock waves when it deleted those words in *BFM2000*. That deletion reflects a narrow view of Scripture by people interested in fighting a culture war and determined to return modern society to a cold-hearted worldview.

This is disrespectful of the eternal truth of Scripture. The Bible is a living book and we must reinterpret its truths with each new generation, under the Lordship of God's Living Word, Jesus Christ. We must apply them to situations readers never imagined. Traditional Baptists work to rescue scriptural truth from those who downgrade it to legalism, rather than uplift it to grace.

Additionally, we must save the purpose of the Scripture from those who use it as a weapon—a club to beat people they oppose. Fundamentalist leaders have done this when they have sought to destroy the reputations of those with whom they disagree. They are constantly accusing people of not believing the Bible.

The Bible is meant to instruct and teach us eternal, spiritual truths about God, sin, salvation, and ourselves. We must use the Bible for "teaching, rebuking, correcting, and training in righteousness" (2 Tim 3:16). Rebuking and correcting do not mean to destroy—rather to enlighten, learn, grow, and deepen. The Bible needs to be rescued from those who use it to divide rather than unite.

. . . Because Baptists believe in freedom.

The genius of the Baptist faith is freedom. Freedom is the reason Baptists have been effective partners with God in reconciling the world unto him. Jesus told us that the truth shall set us free. Jesus said, "I am the way and the truth and the life" (John 14:6).

What is the truth that sets us free? Two pillars of Baptist authority are Jesus Christ and the Scriptures. If we stand firm on the person of Christ and the Scripture, the result is freedom, not creedalism.

Traditional Baptists resist fundamentalism for the sake of freedom given to us through our relationship with Christ and promised to us in God's written Word. Traditional Baptists must resist creedalism because freedom in Christ is the secret to our success as God's partners. We must preserve freedom or the Baptist vision will die!

Fundamentalists accuse traditional Baptists of having no standards because we believe in freedom. Nothing could be further from the truth. Our standard is Jesus Christ revealed in Scripture. The Baptist way builds checks and balances into its structure to take corrective measures when freedom goes beyond Scripture. To stifle freedom is to stifle the genius of the Baptist way.

What are the freedoms traditional Baptists treasure? I give my version of these, acknowledging that Baptist historian Walter Shurden described them better than anyone in his book published by Smyth & Helwys, *The Baptist Identity: The Four Fragile Freedoms*.

1. Bible Freedom: We are people of the Book. Historically, we have never required allegiance to a humanly crafted document such as a faith statement or loyalty oath. The modern SBC has a loyalty oath—the 2000 *Baptist Faith and Message*. Unless you sign it, you cannot serve on any SBC agency board or institution, teach in any SBC seminary, or serve on any SBC mission field. Alarmingly, that sends a loud and clear message from the framers of *BFM2000*—the Bible is not enough!

Reformers resisted creeds of their day and demanded *"Scripture alone"* as their authority. *BFM2000* claims itself to be an "instrument of doctrinal accountability." No authentic Baptist would ever dream of such a thing.

2. Individual Freedom: The priesthood of each believer is critical to Baptist effectiveness. It means God can call, lead, and direct anyone in specific situations for specific ministries anywhere. It means we are all ministers.

What will happen to evangelism when fundamentalists vest all authority in the pastor and do not challenge laypeople to be ministers? We resist fundamentalism for the sake of evangelism! Without the priesthood of each believer, Baptist evangelism will die.

When Richard Jackson was pastor of North Phoenix Baptist Church in Arizona, he baptized more than 20,000 people. Laypeople led most of them to Christ, not Jackson, because he taught them to be authentic Baptists.

Baptists will die if we do not focus on individual evangelism. I challenge Baptists to make it a priority in our churches because God has ordained some to be evangelists. Preach Jesus and challenge people to share their faith as God gives opportunities.

3. Local Church Freedom: This principle gives us the genius of creativity. Churches should not look alike, worship alike, or minister alike. Church members have different gifts and different purposes. We must resist control and conformity because that stifles spreading the kingdom of God. The kingdom needs all kinds of Baptists.

4. Religious Freedom: John Leland, according to Baptist historian William Estep, fought for religious liberty because ninety Baptist ministers and laypeople were imprisoned in colonial Virginia for preaching the gospel. Leland called for absolute religious liberty. He wrote, "Let every man speak freely without fear, maintain the principles that he believes, worship according to his own faith, one God, three Gods, no God, or twenty Gods; and let government protect him in so doing."[2]

George Truett said, "God desires free worshipers and no others." If we do not preserve this truth in Baptist life, who will?

We ground our commitment to religious liberty first in our commitment to evangelism. We want the freedom to preach Jesus anywhere, anytime, within the bounds of religious civility. Many fundamentalists attack religious freedom because they want to use the state's power to promote Jesus and to enforce and spread faith. Authentic Baptists want freedom from the state to preach Jesus. That's a huge difference.

I also want to emphasize freedom overall. Traditional Baptists must defend and make freedom a key emphasis of Baptists nationally. Freedom is essential to fulfilling the call and challenge God has given us.

We can be successful only as free Baptists, not creedal Baptists. As creedal Baptists, we will have no creativity, Spirit, or power. As creedal Baptists, we will ultimately die as a movement. God has given us an unbelievable challenge. God is asking us to preserve the Baptist vision in America and in our missionary endeavors around the world. He wants us to do this for the sake of the gospel and ministry of Jesus Christ.

All of us traditional Baptists do what we do because we owe so much more to God and his Word than legalists will ever see. We cannot compromise Jesus' true character. We cannot compromise the Bible's authority and purpose. Freedom under Christ is essential to being effective partners with God in carrying out the Great Commission to take the gospel to the entire world.

One Baptist vision will dominate the twenty-first century. Will it be the vision of personal judgmentalism, creedalism, and control, or will it be the vision of grace and truth, Jesus, the Bible, and freedom under Christ?

The line is on the ground. Who will step over it?

NOTES

[1] William Barclay, *The Letters to the Galatians and Ephesians, Revised Edition* (Philadelphia: Westminster Press, 1976), 44.

[2] John Leland quoted by Walter Shurden in *The Baptist Identity: Four Fragile Freedoms* (Macon: Smyth & Helwys Publishing, Inc.,1993), 50. Shurden cites what Leland wrote in 1791 in his document, "The Rights of Conscience Inalienable."

NO FREEDOM FOR THE SOUL WITH A CREED

BY JAMES M. DUNN

[Ed. Note: A version of this chapter first appeared in Grady C. Cothen and James M. Dunn's book Soul Freedom: Baptist Battle Cry *published by Smyth & Helwys in 2000.]*

> Baptists are a
> funny breed,
> A churchly crowd
> without a creed.
> It is so.

A creed *prescribes* while a confession of faith *describes* one's approach to religion. A creed is the necessary requirement to squeeze in and squeak by some theological gate.

We Baptists previously have had no catechistic tests for believers. No acceptance of four or four hundred spiritual laws gets one right with God. Neither does swearing allegiance to the 2000 *Baptist Faith and Message*. Repentance and faith, a personal experience of God's grace—not intellectual assent to arguments—saves. It is a spiritual transaction. God's spirit is involved. We have no moral creed.

Even believing and behaving according to code is not in itself redemptive. We "do right" because we *have been* saved not *to be* saved. We certainly should have no political creed. That is in large measure what produced the first Baptists by that name, a dogged dedication to religious freedom.

Non-creedalism drives some folks mad. Always has. The apostle Paul had that problem with early Christians in Galatia. He called them stupid, senseless, foolish, idiots (various translations of Galatians 3:1). He reminded them that "it is precisely for freedom that Christ has set you free" (Galatians 5:1)—soul freedom backed up biblically.

Then in Galatians 5:12, he suggested radical surgery for the legalist who could not live without a rulebook religion. Then and now, rationalism reduces religion to rules. Those who clung to the past saw Paul as a no-law man, an antinomian. Their twenty-first-century successors still libel with labels, striking out at those whom they do not understand. A living faith is hard to take. It just literally drives some people crazy.

Creedlessness makes some true believers sad. He said, "I just cannot believe a thing I cannot understand." Poor little fellow.

One's bucket of religion and spirituality is very small if it holds only what one "knows." In the mix of faith and reason, reason has a useful role. It explains or tries to, interprets, sells, and sometimes satisfies. However, if one's capacity for the divine dimension is limited by rational bounds, his or her pail is too small. There are tons of spiritual stuff none of us can get our puny minds around. Whether limited by scientism like some liberals or by rational fundamentalism like some conservatives, the creed-chained character is pitiable.

A binding creed can turn pious people bad. The philosopher Paschal said, "Men never do evil so fully, so happily, as when they do it for conscience's sake."

One need look at any day's lead news stories to see how hatred, hostility, and violence feed on religious fundamentalism. Other factors—economic, political, and cultural—are involved, but rigid religion makes people as mean as Tasmanian Devils out of otherwise decent disciples. Look at the Middle East, the Balkans, India, Northern Ireland, and on and on. Who wants to fight and kill over propositions in the light of the grace God offers?

A living faith not bound by creed makes Baptists glad. It's love not law, faith not fact, persons not propositions, experience with God not expectations of persons at the heart of free and faithful Baptists and all believers of whatever brand. In the blessed absence of a creed the confession of faith common to Baptists looms large: Jesus Christ is Lord. That ancient confession is historically potent, theologically eclectic, spiritually significant, religiously accessible, biblically sound, and humanly available.

It is enough.

How can a creedless Christianity avoid "I-come-to-the-garden-alone" subjective religion? Doesn't faith without a rational checklist become nothing more than C. S. Lewis' "tickle around the gizzard"? Can a rope of sand bind together believers of the same bent?

Dangers abound. Soul freedom is a risky route. Experiment is close to the essence of experiential Christianity.

Yet, the risks are worth taking. The very meaning of "faith" is inextricably entangled in the Baptist brand of belief that insists upon an intimate individual religious commitment. We stay under the umbrella of traditional Christianity. So far, at least, we Baptists have gotten by with this perilous practice of soul freedom with four substantial flying buttresses propping up the churches.

One is a radical Christ-centrism, the Christian doctrine, growing out of the radical monotheism that makes us such soul brothers and sisters with Jewish friends. That high and practical Christology takes seriously the words from 1 Timothy 2:5, "one mediator between God and all humankind." The same noble notion of an immanent and immediate friendship with Jesus sometimes slides into "WWJD" ethical temperature-taking. That's inadequate.

Then, there is, has been, is likely to be a reliance upon the Bible. Even a "liberal Baptist," an oxymoron, insists upon the authority of Scripture and argues that the written record of God's revelation is the "sole rule for faith and practice." The failure to buy the buzz word "inerrancy" hardly makes anyone a Bible-basher.

Another support for the centrality of soul freedom is the insistence on and acceptance of a regenerate church membership. If, indeed, one touts soul freedom for herself, she cannot escape granting it to all other born-again believers. This builds a fellowship of mutual respect, acceptance, and shared pilgrimage. Church members can support, empathize, even admonish and correct one another.

Finally, it must be admitted that one of the safeguards against utter subjectivism on the part of free souls has been the social system, the cultural props, the common-denominator identity that all Christians have in the civil-religion-shaped nation. A culture-wide comfort zone has shielded many believers of all stripes from hard questions and tough decisions about their personal faith. The day in which one could say, "Of course I'm a Christian—I'm an American, aren't I?" is gone.

The pluralism, multi-culturalism, and secularism (at its best and at its worst) that we know today requires us to rethink our deepest held beliefs. Soul freedom is certainly one of those beliefs for Baptists.

That soul freedom demands personal interaction and responsibility. Abstract propositions, however true or however close to The Truth, are not enough.

"I know whom I have believed." That's the Scripture (2 Timothy 1:12). Those are the words of the 1883 gospel song by Daniel W. Whittle, not "I know *what* I believe."

J. M. Dawson, first executive of the Baptist Joint Committee, once told me that he and George W. Truett consider themselves "Christian personalists." That terminology seems odd today, but the need for that brand of believer is great.

In fact, one cannot comprehend historic Baptists' passion for religious liberty without catching the intensely personal fever of their faith. It's not so much whether their beliefs are literal or liberal as that they are personal that counts.

The intensely personal nature of biblical faith is a Baptist birthmark. Frank Louis Mauldin has tried to help us catch on in *The Classic Baptist Heritage of Personal Truth* (Providence House Publishers, 1999); "The Truth as It Is in Jesus" is the subtitle. The book

23

contributes significantly to understanding Baptists and our hot-eyed, narrow-minded, loud-mouthed defense of religious liberty and her theological sister, soul freedom.

We have no book quite like this one. It examines and celebrates the biblical and the historic Baptist understanding of personal truth. We have books that explain Baptist faith and practice, others that consider Baptist history, and still more that examine a particular theological or denominational issue. But no other book undertakes the avowed fourfold purpose of (1) identifying and analyzing the distinctive notion of personal truth, (2) demonstrating the existence of a classic Baptist heritage of truth, (3) understanding what it means for Baptists in the classic heritage to equate truth with "the truth that is in Jesus," and (4) making the case that the story of personal truth (along with the stories of faith and freedom) constitutes the soul—the essential core and the common ground—of Baptist identity and integrity.

I heard a propositionalist testify: "I just cannot believe anything that I cannot understand." In this book Mauldin offers an antidote for that faith-threatening poison. The book and its biblical concept of incarnational truth also save us from the ditches on either side of the Christian way: *sola scriptura* on one side and *sola fide* on the other.

Mauldin documents and demonstrates that Baptists have always majored on experiential religion informed by the "Holy Word of God" and quickened by God's Spirit. The author says it all when he affirms that "Baptists...defend the thesis that truth is someone real, not something true." Jesus said, "I am the way, the truth and the life." One who reads this book may discover what a Baptist is.

Baptists are not alone in this dogged focus on personal faith. In 1972, Richard R. Niebuhr probed and provided a theoretical basis for belief, for affection rooted in religious experience. In the afterword of his book *Experiential Religion* he writes, "Human faith is not so much a sum of answers as it is a way of seeing and acting, and books about faith have first of all to describe what faithful men see and believe to be real."

Mauldin brings us one of those "books about faith" which does just that. John P. Newport in his foreword to the book calls it "a unique and important book." Newport acknowledges that Professor Mauldin's "emphasis on the fact that biblical truth is relational is very important."

Walter B. Shurden hits the same note, but denies that Baptist personalism is privatism or "Lone Ranger" religion. "To insist," says Shurden, "that saving faith is personal not impersonal, relational not ritualistic, direct not indirect, private not corporate has never meant for Baptists that the Christian life is a privatized disengagement from either the church or society." Even Walter Rauschenbush, father of the *Social Gospel*, gave 'experimental religion' as his first reason for being Baptist. Authentic faith requires soul freedom. One who has maneuvered and manipulated to mouth some counterfeit confession not profoundly personal is in danger of losing his immortal soul.

It's *who*, not *what*, we believe that makes us Christian.

AN EDITOR VIEWS THE
BFM2000'S IMPACT ON BAPTISTS

BY JOHN D. PIERCE

Baptist editors chose the controversial revisions to the *Baptist Faith and Message* statement as the top news story of 2000 in an annual survey by the independent news service Associated Baptist Press (ABP). The impact and implications of those revisions have continued to make news.

The first controversy related to altering the 1963 faith statement came two years before the 2000 revisions. Messengers to the 1998 Southern Baptist Convention (SBC) meeting in Salt Lake City, Utah, approved the addition of an article on "the family" that went beyond affirming Christian marriage, responsible sexuality, and the priority of parenting. Although stating that the "husband and wife are of equal worth before God," the article added: "A wife is to submit herself graciously to the servant leadership of her husband . . ."

Proponents of the article said the statement simply reflected the distinct roles of husbands and wives as described in Ephesians 5:24. Critics argued that those drafting the article ignored verse 21 that calls for mutual submission.

The words "graciously submit" were immediately and widely used in serious debates as well as humorous references concerning the controversial addition to the *BFM*.

Messengers easily approved the so-called "family article," which some observers consider the first of several actions taken by Southern Baptists in recent years to restrict the influence of women in church and society.

Ensuing changes in SBC agencies and institutions have included altering seminary training for women, refusing to endorse vocational female chaplains who have been ordained by a local church, and rewording the 2000 *Baptist Faith and Message* (*BFM2000*) to affirm that only men are biblically qualified to serve as "senior pastors."

The family article was added in 1998, the same year Paige Patterson, president of Southeastern Baptist Theological Seminary in Wake Forest, NC, and a chief architect of the fundamentalist takeover of the SBC, was elected SBC president.

A headline in the Texas Baptist newspaper, the *Baptist Standard*, following the annual SBC meeting, read: "SBC puts Patterson, women in place."After a complaint from Baptist Press, the official news service of the SBC, then-managing editor Marv Knox (now the editor) apologized for wording the headline that way. However, many observers considered it to be accurate, and just the beginning of a broader effort to minimize the role of women in SBC life.

Although the *BFM2000* identifies only the office of "senior pastor," a relatively new term in most Baptist churches, as being off limits to women, the document has been applied more broadly. Cases have arisen occasionally where the revised faith statement has been evoked to refute women ministers who hold leadership roles or ministry positions other than that of pastor, and to condemn churches that choose to ordain women.

The Council on Biblical Manhood and Womanhood, an organization active on The Southern Baptist Theological Seminary campus in Louisville, Kentucky, promotes the positions added to the *BFM* in 1998 and 2000 concerning the role of women in marital relationships and in church leadership.

Words and deeds of many current Southern Baptist leaders at the national, state, and associational levels give evidence of a strong resistance to women who acknowledge a call to ministry and to the churches that ordain and affirm them.

NEWS SPIKES

The addition of the family article to the *BFM* in 1998 brought considerable news coverage from both the religious and secular media, as did the major revision of the statement by messengers at the Orlando SBC annual meeting in the summer of 2000.

While experienced religion writers usually got the fuller picture, television and radio reports (as well as some newspapers) focused almost exclusively on the opposition to women pastors. Some secular journalists even wrongly concluded that the SBC has the authority to prohibit women from serving in pastoral roles, not understanding that each Baptist church retains local control in calling a minister.

It was interesting, and a bit amusing, to watch secular reporters interview critics of the changes in the *BFM2000* who articulated their concerns over removing the "christological criterion" for interpreting Scripture or other theological issues related to the revised statement. There was little chance that the fast-writing reporters would comprehend the scribbled words and almost none that they would appear on the evening news or in the morning paper.

Revisions to the *BFM*, however, had not consistently dominated Baptist news publications in recent years before a renewed flurry in 2002. Rather, they had surfaced at various times when the statement was adopted by another Baptist body or used by SBC agencies or institutions as a requirement for employment. Addition of the family article in 1998 and the major revision in 2000 had kept the attention of journalists—and readers, we assume—for several weeks.

In the fall of 2000, related stories appeared as state conventions responded in various ways to the faith statement at their annual meetings. Some state Baptist bodies (including Florida, Georgia, Missouri, Louisiana, Colorado, and Oklahoma) affirmed the *BFM2000* or officially adopted it as their own faith statement. Other state conventions embraced it along with earlier Baptist confessions, or reinforced their approval of the 1963 version, or limited their affirmation to the Bible alone, or did not consider the issue at all, or—in good Baptist fashion—established a committee to study the situation.

News stories have also arisen when trustees of SBC agencies and institutions have adopted the *BFM2000* and enforced adherence to it as a qualification for employment. By requiring SBC employees to sign the more narrow doctrinal statement, fundamentalist trustees obtained a new method for weeding out those workers they consider more moderate in their theological leanings and/or less than enthusiastic supporters of the SBC takeover.

Some who left denominational positions as a result of these policies cited disagreement with such revisions as those on a woman's role at home and in church, removal of Jesus Christ as the criterion through which Scripture is interpreted, use of the *BFM* as an "instrument of doctrinal accountability," and what they perceived as a violation of freedom. Interestingly, some of those leaving seminary faculties had just been hired a few years earlier because they were conservative scholars who embraced the concept of biblical inerrancy that fundamentalist leaders had touted as the essential requirement for Southern Baptist teachers.

Fundamentalist Baptist leaders committed to the two-decade shift in the Convention have solidly controlled all SBC agencies and institutions for several years. Pragmatism, however, does break through occasionally.

At Southeastern Seminary, for example, trustees required signing of the *BFM2000* for newly hired faculty only. Current faculty could voluntarily comply. The action allowed long-time missions professor George Braswell—who likely would not have signed the statement—to complete the establishment of a new overseas doctoral program for the seminary before retiring.

Then, in early 2002, news coverage hit the front page once again and kept escalating during a series of actions involving the two mission boards and the SBC Executive Committee.

The International and North American Mission Boards (IMB and NAMB) asked their missionaries to sign the *BFM2000*, and the North American Mission Board refused to endorse ordained women as chaplains. Meanwhile, the autonomous District of Columbia Baptist Convention refused a NAMB directive to submit to its administrative control, and Morris Chapman, Executive Committee president and CEO, refused to recognize or take funds from a newly formed moderate convention that split from the Missouri Baptist Convention after a fundamentalist takeover there. The Executive Committee, however, recognizes fundamentalist conventions that have split off the older Virginia and Texas Baptist state bodies.

Jerry Rankin, president of the IMB, launched the news flurry with a letter to all veteran Southern Baptist missionaries overseas, asking them to sign a statement affirming their adherence to the *BFM2000*. That action, already required of newly appointed missionaries, was necessary, he said, to silence unnamed critics who are "suspicious" of some missionaries' doctrinal soundness. It was an administrative decision, Rankin said, but one widely believed by others to come from pressure from some trustees and other key fundamentalist leaders.

Rankin's decision reversed his earlier promises that assured Southern Baptist missionaries that their thorough screening process and years of faithful service were enough to prove their doctrinal trustworthiness. His decision also struck a nerve of many mission-minded Baptists who began to realize that two decades of fundamentalist dominance now affected their beloved missions force. That escalated a continuing backlash.

News soon followed from the NAMB that all its fully funded national missionaries were also being called on to sign the *BFM2000*. The action came as no surprise, but the revelation that less than sixty persons, fully funded by NAMB, serve in these roles was news to many Southern Baptists.

A CASE FOR CHANGE

Those who drafted, proposed, and supported the revisions to the *BFM* built their case largely on the fact that Southern Baptists had set a precedent by updating the 1925 version in 1963, and on their perception that society has changed considerably since then.

In making their report to the SBC in Orlando, the committee that drafted the revised statement spoke to the issue of changes and challenges:

> New challenges to faith appear in every age. . . . Now, faced with a culture hostile to the very notion of truth, this generation of Baptists must claim anew the eternal truths of the Christian faith. (Report of the *Baptist Faith and Message* Study Committee, 14 June 2000.)

An overwhelming majority of the nearly 12,000 messengers voted to approve the report. Prior to the vote, the committee restored the terms "priesthood of believer" and "soul competency" to the new preamble after hearing many express concerns about the removal of historic Baptist principles.

However, both the committee and the majority of messengers rejected attempts to restore a statement that affirms Jesus Christ as the criterion by which Scripture is interpreted. A heated debate on the authority of Scripture consumed much of the allotted time for debating the revised faith statement.

Charles Wade, executive director of the Baptist General Convention of Texas (BGCT), who offered one of the failed amendments from the floor, asked if Jesus is not the criterion for biblical interpretation, then who or what is? But proponents of removing the statement argued that moderate Baptists have used it in a way that lessens biblical authority. Other Baptists have responded that a legalistic approach also diminishes biblical authority and that removing Jesus Christ as the criterion for interpreting Scripture diminishes his Lordship.

Though the *BFM2000* tightened up language about biblical authority and affirmed that the Scriptures are "totally true and trustworthy," the committee chose not to use the term "inerrant" to describe the Bible. Its omission is noteworthy because it was the most used term by fundamentalists who claimed that the SBC had experienced a "liberal drift" that required them to orchestrate the takeover of the Convention that began in 1979.

As a result of the convincing vote to approve the *BFM2000*, SBC leaders routinely speak of these doctrinal positions as representing the vast majority of Southern Baptists. Whether or not the theological views of most Baptists in the pews are consistent with those who gathered in Orlando in the summer of 2000 is not actually known.

Several Baptist editors were considering, as this book was going to press, linking with a respected independent research company to determine if indeed the doctrinal positions articulated in the latest faith statement are consistent with most Southern Baptists. Many Baptists would argue, however, that in the light of Baptist history and diversity, room should be left for the individual priesthood of the believer, despite the numbers involved.

CRITICS ASSAIL CHANGES

Critics of the latest changes to the *BFM* have offered numerous opinions as to why they find the new statement to be at least inadequate—if not offensive. Arguments generally address three aspects of the revised statement or the process by which it was developed.

The first area of criticism has to do with the political nature of the committee charged with drafting the revisions. Former SBC President Adrian Rogers was named chair by Paige Patterson, who held the office at the time.

The remaining committee, appointed by Patterson, was characterized as "diverse" because members came from various states. It included two women and some ethnic diversity was evident. However, all members were clearly strong supporters of the fundamentalist direction of the SBC. Southern Seminary President Albert Mohler was considered the primary writer, or "the Thomas Jefferson," as one supporter put it, of the revised statement.

The 1963 committee, on the other hand, was comprised of elected presidents from the various state conventions that brought together a wider sampling of theological positions. Critics argued that a similar approach would have more accurately represented Southern Baptist thought.

Critics also suggested that the goals of the two committees were vastly different. The 1963 committee sought to determine broadly shared beliefs of most Southern Baptists as a way of communicating these beliefs to outsiders. The statement was often described as an "umbrella" under which a large, diverse body of Baptist Christians could stand.

The 2000 committee, critics argued, sought to narrowly define a more fundamentalist doctrine as a way of excluding fellow Southern Baptists from participation in SBC life who could never agree with those positions.

A second area of criticism relates specifically to the changes in the document itself. The ones garnering the most attention are related to the authority of the *BFM* vs. the Bible, the role of Jesus Christ as the criterion for interpreting Scripture, and the role of women.

The assertion that the Bible disqualifies women from pastoral ministry has been criticized as both a misinterpretation of Scripture and as an intrusion into the autonomy of local churches.

The third aspect of the faith statement that has drawn criticism is the way in which the *BFM2000* has been used. Lengthy debates have been ensued over the differences in "confessions" and "creeds" and whether requiring employees and appointees to sign a document locking in doctrinal positions is a responsible oversight or a violation of their freedom.

In presenting its report, the committee described confessions of faith as "instruments of doctrinal accountability." That specific wording is in the *BFM2000* preamble.

Critics argue that such authority is too strong for Baptists, who have historically held confessional statements to be non-binding descriptions of widely held Baptist beliefs.

They argue that leaving no latitude for other interpretations flies in the face of Baptist history; it removes the priesthood of the individual believer from the equation and replaces it with a corporate interpretation of the priesthood; it turns a confession of faith into a binding creed.

A DOCTRINAL DIVIDE

The SBC's Convention Press published a book in 1971 simply titled, *The Baptist Faith and Message.* Author Herschel H. Hobbs of Oklahoma, a respected conservative theologian who chaired the committee that drafted the 1963 revision of the faith statement, expanded on its various articles.

In the preface, Hobbs carefully clarified that "in no sense is this work a binding statement of faith and message for Southern Baptists." He was also cautious in stating that he personally, though a Southern Baptist, did not pretend to speak on behalf of all others.

Rather, he described his writings as "one Baptist's effort to interpret a statement which Southern Baptist messengers in assembled session voted as comprising a treatment of faith generally agreed upon by Southern Baptists."

Hobbs's efforts to diminish the document's authority and to resist using it as a measuring stick for orthodoxy are a stark contrast to the framers of the more narrow 2000 document. Following its adoption, the latter statement has been strongly defended as truth by its drafters and denounced by opponents as "an instrument of doctrinal accountability" that restricts participation in the SBC.

More than any other person, Hobbs's hand was all over the 1963 statement. Yet he expressed only a desire that his efforts would "prove helpful in enabling others to understand more fully the Baptist faith and message," and he urged fellow Baptists to search the Scriptures themselves under the guidance of the Holy Spirit in the constant pursuit of divine truth.

Hobbs also wrote in 1971, "Baptists are an amazing people . . . (who) have no creed, yet enjoy a remarkable unity."

Three decades later, the deep division among those who once comprised the Southern Baptist Convention reflects anything but unity. Many would also argue that indeed the SBC now has a creed—and it is one of the reasons that "remarkable unity" is no longer a proper term for describing Southern Baptists as they have previously been known.

A SERIOUS LOOK AT THE *BAPTIST FAITH AND MESSAGE* REVISIONS

BY RUSSELL H. DILDAY

In the late 1970s, a well-organized, well-financed cadre of ultra-conservatives launched a crusade to win control of the Southern Baptist Convention (SBC). It was a simple, but effective plan: circulate exaggerated and unproven "evidences" that the Southern Baptist Convention was drifting into theological liberalism. This would arouse the fears of like-minded Baptists—especially pastors of smaller churches who might already feel left out, and laypersons who had limited knowledge of denominational matters. Then, using secular political tactics, organize these concerned Baptists into "precincts" across the various Southern Baptist state conventions. Ask each precinct to enlist messengers from their churches willing to attend the annual convention meeting, vote the party line, and thereby "save the SBC" by turning it "back to the Bible."

Transportation and hotel rooms would be arranged, and in some cases paid for. Usually they would not need the rooms because the well-rehearsed messengers would attend only one crucial business session—the one where their candidate for convention president was to be elected. After that vote, the bus or the car pool would take the crusaders back home. Although founded on exaggerated, unsubstantiated "evidences," the plan would enlist enough votes to elect the president by narrow margins in a succession of annual meetings. Since the SBC president makes the appointments that control the naming of trustees of the seminaries and other convention institutions, the political organizers would seize control of the entire denominational structure in only a few years.

The strategy worked. By the 1990s the fundamentalist organizers had put themselves into positions of leadership, and they are now in control of Convention decision-making. During the past ten years, these new SBC leaders have radically changed the denomination's institutions and agencies, and are now solidifying their political successes by rewriting the convention's history from their perspective and by revising the SBC's faith statement to reflect their narrow ultra-conservative beliefs.

SBC CONFESSIONS OF FAITH: A HISTORICAL REVIEW

In 1998 and again in 2000, high profile personalities in the "takeover" party of the convention engineered significant revisions in the Southern Baptist Convention's confession of faith, which is the only doctrinal statement the SBC had for 153 years, up to 1998.

First approved in 1925, and given only minor editorial revisions in 1963, this confession of faith, called the *Baptist Faith and Message* (*BFM1925* and *BFM1963*), had been considered adequate in the convention until theological hard-liners gained the ascendancy.

Now, for the first time in SBC history, the most recently revised version of this statement of faith (*BFM2000*) is being used as an official creed to enforce loyalty to the party in power. Not only are seminary professors and missionaries expected to endorse the *BFM2000*, but SBC leaders are also applying pressure on state conventions, associations, and even local congregations to give their assent. Those who refuse risk isolation or even expulsion from the denominational circle.

Historically, Southern Baptists have had an aversion to creeds—even to less threatening confessions of faith. When the convention was organized in Augusta, Georgia, in 1845, the messengers agreed:

> We have constructed for our basis no new creed, acting in this matter upon a
> Baptist aversion for all creeds except the Bible.[1]

Eighty years later in 1925, in an attempt to settle a controversy, the SBC reluctantly adopted its first confession of faith. Basing it largely on the New Hampshire Confession of 1833, the framers carefully pointed out that the statement was merely a "confession" of what most messengers at the annual meeting understood to be the general beliefs of Baptists. The preamble made it clear in 1925, and again when minor editorial revisions were made in 1963, that the statement was not intended to be a creed, nor was it to be used to enforce conformity of belief:

> Confessions are only guides in interpretation, having no authority over the
> conscience . . . they are not to be used to hamper freedom of thought or inves-
> tigation in other realms of life.[2]

The 1925 confession was approved by a vast majority of the messengers, but, as historian W. W. Barnes reported, "It was received by the churches with a loud outburst of silence." The constituency largely ignored it because they rightly understood it be a non-binding expression of one group of Baptists meeting in one session of one annual convention. It might be useful as a consensus statement of widely held convictions, but it had no authority whatsoever.

The 1963 version received more attention, but it was still circulated as an incomplete and fallible "consensus of opinion":

> They are statements of religious convictions, drawn from the Scriptures, and are not to be used to hamper freedom of thought or investigation in other realms of life.[3]

Baptists have always claimed that their only creed is the Bible and, until recently, they have defended tenaciously the privilege of every believer, with the illumination of the Holy Spirit, to interpret Scripture according to his or her own conscience. This deeply engrained anti-creedal sentiment, so characteristic of Baptists, lies behind the negative reactions to the newly revised confession and its use as a tool to enforce doctrinal uniformity.

Some are understandably suspicious of *BFM2000* merely because the "party," which engineered the two-decade scheme to take control of the SBC, crafted it. The revision committee was made up exclusively of those sympathetic with the convention's new direction, and, as a matter of fact, most were active players in the crusade to control and redirect the SBC.

One Baptist editor describes the implied scenario that engenders this suspicion of the *BFM2000*:

> Twenty-one years ago a master plan for the repositioning of the SBC would have looked something like this. Elect SBC presidents sympathetic to fiercely conservative principles. Appoint like-minded trustees to govern SBC institutions. Hire to the staffs of convention agencies, employees who buy into the SBC's rightward shift. Create a new SBC infrastructure that reflects a more conservative direction. Rewrite the history of this era with the victor's spin. Revise the SBC theological statement, the 1963 *Baptist Faith and Message*, to codify the new, more fundamental, direction of the SBC. With the release of the report of the Committee on the *Baptist Faith and Message* . . . , the final stage of this re-imaging is set in motion.[4]

It is not surprising, then, that reactions to the statement have largely followed political alignments—those who support the new convention leadership and direction favor the document, and those who oppose what they call "the takeover of the SBC" challenge the document.

POSITIVE FACTORS IN THE 2000 REVISION

Admittedly, there are certain positive elements in *BFM2000*, and they should be acknowledged, even though some of them raise questions.

1. To the surprise of many, the committee did not insert the controversial language of "inerrancy" into the section on Scripture, which would have further divided the constituency. The omission does seem curious, since so much of the twenty-year controversy centered on enforcing the use of the term "inerrant" to describe the nature of the Bible. Does that mean the term is no longer deemed necessary? Was it a real issue all those years, or just a semantic difference used as a "smoke screen" for a power grab, as many believe? While holding a high view of Scripture through the years, Baptists have historically shunned the term "inerrant" and have chosen instead to use such terms as "true," "inspired," and "authoritative." Many fundamentalists still insist on "inerrancy" as a measure of acceptability, but it was not inserted into *BFM2000*.

2. Neither did the revisers insert more restrictive views of eschatology (the doctrine of last things), such as dispensational pre-millennialism, as some had feared. During the fundamentalist attack on the convention, seminary professors who did not affirm dispensational eschatology were criticized as liberals and were cited as examples of why the takeover was necessary. But, again, this was now not considered important enough to include. (It is telling, however, to note that many of the recent faculty additions, including the new provost, at Southwestern Baptist Theological Seminary in Fort Worth, Texas, are graduates of Dallas Theological Seminary, a recognized center of dispensational interpretation.)

3. At the last minute, following growing criticism of its deletion in their first draft, the committee did strengthen the document by reinserting a statement that Baptists honor the principles of soul competency and the priesthood of believers. However, critics point out that their substitution of the plural form "believers" distorts the true meaning of the "priesthood of each believer" (see "troubling factor" number 2 in this chapter).

4. Apart from some very controversial sections, which are addressed in this chapter, the rest of the revised statement does reaffirm other basic Baptist doctrines found in *BFM1963*. Baptists have typically expressed their convictions boldly and clearly, unlike theological minimalists in some mainline groups who adopt cultural trends as church polity and embrace broad spectrums of belief instead of making critical theological distinctions. If Baptists needed another example of the courage to express convictions, then *BFM2000* addresses that need.

5. The new document does speak to issues that the revisers consider to be of contemporary concern—exclusivism versus inclusivism (Section IV) related to soteriology (the doctrine of salvation), family (Section XVIII), gender (Section III), sexual immorality, adultery, homosexuality, pornography, and abortion (Section XV). However, the inclusion of such current specifics to the exclusion of others can also be seen as a weakness (see "troubling factor" number 9).

6. It closes ranks and defines the new version of the SBC more specifically, so it can clearly be understood, either by those who agree or those who disagree. If there remains any

ambiguity about the future direction of the SBC under its current hard-line leadership, this document unflinchingly clears the air. The revisions in *BFM2000* clearly reveal where the SBC under its new leadership is headed.

7. Some editorial changes, such as the use of gender-inclusive language, improve the form of the statement.

TROUBLING FACTORS IN THE 2000 REVISION

Negative criticisms of *BFM2000* seem to cluster around twelve issues:

1. The deletion of the Christocentric criterion for interpretation of Scripture.
2. The diminishing of the doctrines of soul competency and the priesthood of the believer.
3. The trend toward creedalism.
4. The diminishing of the doctrine of autonomy and freedom of the local church under the leadership of the Holy Spirit.
5. The trend toward "five-point" Calvinism and the attendant mistrust of personal Christian experience.
6. The trend shifting Baptist identity from its Anabaptist, Free Church tradition to a reformed evangelical identity.
7. The narrow interpretation of the role of women in marriage.
8. The narrow interpretation of the role of women in the church.
9. The "Pandora's box" concern—a fear of repeated future revisions to include a wide variety of favorite opinions.
10. The false accusation of neo-orthodoxy in the content of *BFM1963*.
11. The trend toward including a catalogue of specific current sins.
12. Inconsistency.

1. The deletion of the christocentric criterion for interpretation of Scripture.

BFM1963 says:
> "The criterion by which the Bible is to be interpreted is Jesus Christ."

BFM2000 substituted:
> "All Scripture is a testimony to Christ, who is himself the focus of divine revelation."

BFM2000 also deleted from *BFM1963*:
> "Baptists are a people who profess a living faith. This faith is rooted and grounded in Jesus Christ who is the same yesterday, and today, and forever. Therefore, the sole

37

authority for faith and practice among Baptists is Jesus Christ whose will is revealed in the Holy Scriptures".

The revision intentionally rejects an important hermeneutical principle. Baptists (and most evangelicals) have valued what is called the "theological principal" of biblical interpretation. This principle teaches that the Bible is a book of faith, not just history or philosophy. Therefore, the Bible cannot be fully understood from the outside by grammar, logic, rhetoric, and history alone. It must be understood from its center—Jesus Christ. This biblical center yields itself best to those who have a personal relationship with God through Jesus Christ and whose interpretations are enlightened by the Holy Spirit.

This "theological principle," expressed in the christocentric language of *BFM1963* ("The criterion by which the Bible is to be interpreted is Jesus Christ"), declares that the guiding key to biblical interpretation is the Lord Jesus Christ. Through Him as a criterion, or standard, we understand the Bible to be unified, self-consistent, and coherent.

Jesus said, "The Scriptures . . . bear witness to me" (John 5:39). Therefore, we are to interpret the Old Testament and the rest of the Bible in the light of the life and teachings of Jesus in the New Testament, illuminated by our own direct experience with the living Christ. Through Jesus as the criterion, we interpret the prophecies and the ceremonial, civil, dietary, and moral laws of the Old Testament.

Martin Luther was right in insisting that the Bible must always be understood from its center—its heart—its Christ. As British theologian Alan P. F. Sell puts it:

> All our talk about God must be anchored in what we know of him in Christ; otherwise, we shall arrive at an unworthy view of God. Why do we say of our God that he is love and not hate? Because of what we see in Christ. . . . if we do not begin from the holy love of God made known to us in Christ, we shall find ourselves in difficulties when we come to fill out our understanding of God.[5]

The intentional deletion of this christological principal of biblical interpretation is, to many, the most serious flaw in *BFM2000*. It appears to elevate the Bible above Jesus and ignores the fact that He is not only "the focus of divine revelation" but is also Lord of the Bible. Concerned critics say:

> "This amounts to nothing less than idolatry . . ."
> "It is pure bibliolatry. . ."
> "I'll bow down to King Jesus, but I will never bow down to King James."[6]

The revisers defended their deletion in a press release on June 5, 2000:

> This statement (Jesus is the criterion) was controversial because some have used it to drive a wedge between the incarnate word and the written word and to deny the truthfulness of certain passages.[7]

Ken Hemphill, president of Southwestern Seminary, further explained the deletion of the christocentric criterion, calling it:

> A loophole to avoid the plain teaching of certain biblical texts which persists among moderates. . . . [I]t is used by some unprincipled Baptist scholars to ignore difficult texts, which they did not believe to reflect the character of Jesus.[8]

But surely this crucial christological principle, treasured by Baptists and other evangelical conservatives over the years, should not be abandoned just because some misguided interpreters are said to have abused it.

Reflecting on this change, an editorial in *Christianity Today* claimed *BFM2000*

> is poorer without the rich christocentric language of the earlier statement. Jesus Christ is surely the center of Scripture as well as its Lord. One can affirm this while also welcoming the clear affirmation of the Bible as God's infallible, revealed word.[9]

2. The diminishing of the doctrines of soul competency and the priesthood of the believer.

"Soul competency" is the view that the redemptive and revelatory work of Jesus Christ allows an individual believer to go directly to God through Christ without any human mediator. "The priesthood of the believer" is the view that through Christ each believer—both clergy and laity—is a priest, responsible to God for interpreting and following the Bible and for interceding on behalf others. Both E. Y. Mullins and Herschel Hobbs named "soul competency" the most distinctive doctrine among Baptists.

But Southern Seminary President Al Mohler, a major voice, if not the primary composer, on the revision committee, has recently denounced these two historic Baptist convictions—especially as E. Y. Mullins, a previous Southern Seminary president, espoused them. In his Founder's Day address at the seminary, March 30, 2000, Mohler said that Mullins's emphasis on soul competency has "infected" the SBC with an "autonomous individualism" that undermines biblical authority to this day. He accused President Mullins of steering the SBC off course by making personal Christian experience more important than biblical authority. He warned that soul competency "serves as an acid dissolving religious authority, congregationalism, confessionalism, and mutual theological accountability."[10]

An even stronger condemnation of these two distinctive Baptist doctrines appeared in the Winter 1999 issue of the seminary's theological journal, written by Sean Michael Lucas, associate director Southern Seminary's Center for the Study of the SBC:

> For over 70 years, Southern Baptists have harvested the shallow discipleship and vapid theology that resulted from sowing Mullins' theological seeds of experience. It is time to return to the founders of the SBC trained in the hardy doctrinal tradition of the Princeton theology.

Following this line of thought, *BFM2000* at first deleted the following references to these doctrines in *BFM1963*:

> Baptists emphasize the soul's competency before God, freedom of religion, and the priesthood of the believer. However, this emphasis should not be interpreted to mean that there is an absence of certain definite doctrines that Baptists believe, cherish, and with which they have been and are now closely identified.

But when they discovered the revisers had deleted these words, many Baptists raised an outcry of disapproval. So, less than an hour before the report was brought to the convention for approval, the following was reluctantly reinserted:

> We honor the principles of soul competency and the priesthood of believers, affirming together both our liberty in Christ and our accountability to each other under the Word of God.

While this last-minute reversal was at first welcomed by critics, it was soon discovered that the reinserted wording had been subtly changed. They substituted the plural—"priesthood of believers"—in the place of the singular form in *BFM1963*, "priesthood of the believer." In so doing, the revisers again expressed their mistrust of personal, individual experience, focusing instead on "accountability to each other," undoubtedly referring to an approved denominational belief system.

This in essence rejects the historic Baptist doctrine of the priesthood of each individual believer (singular), replacing it with a more Reformed doctrine of the priesthood of believers (plural). That turns individual priesthood into a corporate priesthood. Al Mohler defended the reinterpretation:

It is dangerous to say the priesthood of the believer. It is not just that we stand alone; it is that we stand together—and we stand together under the authority of God's word.[11]

Other defenders of the revised plural form say the singular wording of *BFM1963* leads to:

a kind of private interpretation which, while adhering to an ambiguously crafted "criterion" of Jesus Christ, eviscerates the biblical doctrines . . . .[12]

But one Baptist editor countered:

While I am content to stand before God under the authority of Scripture, I can do so whether I'm alone or in a crowd of all 15.8 million Southern Baptists. While I appreciate the committee's efforts to at least partially restore a pair of key Baptist doctrines, I am confident it is not dangerous to be a lone priest/believer in the presence of Almighty God through the power of his Holy Spirit.[13]

Many believe that these omissions, reinsertions, and changes show a lack of appreciation for—even a rejection of—two very important Baptist ideals.

3. The trend toward creedalism.

BFM2000 deleted the following passage from *BFM1963* that the framers hoped would protect the 1963 statement from becoming a creed to enforce doctrinal uniformity: "Such statements have never been regarded as complete, infallible statements of faith, nor as official creeds carrying mandatory authority" (from the Preamble).

Furthermore, the revisers inserted in *BFM2000* language never before used in a Southern Baptist confession of faith:

Baptist churches, associations, and general bodies have adopted confessions of faith as a witness to the world, and as *instruments of doctrinal accountability*. We are not embarrassed to state before the world that these are doctrines we hold precious and as *essential to the Baptist tradition of faith and practice*. (From the Introduction, italics mine).

As Jim Denison, pastor of Park Cities Baptist Church, Dallas, Texas, says,

For the first time, the denominational faith statement is intended to be an "instrument of doctrinal accountability." For whom? By whom? . . . And for

> the first time, this faith statement is said to be "essential to the Baptist tradition of faith and practice." Essential for what? For whom? . . . Simply put, a document which elevates such a human statement of faith to this level of authority cannot be understood to be Baptist.[14]

These changes, along with the minimizing of local church autonomy (see "troubling factor" number 4), show that the new SBC is becoming an authoritarian body, an ecclesiastical hierarchy, mandating what local churches must believe and do.

Already, *BFM2000* is being used improperly to restrict representation on SBC committees and boards, and to measure the orthodoxy of associations and local churches. Already, Southern Baptist missionaries are being pressured to endorse the new statement or face uncertain consequences. Already, tensions have arisen in state conventions where SBC representatives are trying to enforce compliance with the new directions of the SBC by pressuring the states to adopt *BFM2000*.

It is no surprise, then, to see this creedal coercion now being aimed at local autonomous congregations. Headlines are being made in Florida and North Carolina where Baptist associations are threatening local churches with dismissal if they do not endorse the *BFM2000*. This should raise the hackles of every true Baptist!

Two related questions arise from the concern over creedalism:

(1) Should seminary professors be required to sign this and any future revised doctrinal statements? Seminaries accredited by the Association of Theological Schools are expected to have a statement of faith as an objective standard by which they evaluate the teaching of professors. The institution's faith statement serves to protect professors from unfounded accusations of heresy. Before the political takeover of the convention, all six of the SBC seminaries had adopted *BFM1963* as their doctrinal guideline. (In the case of Southern Seminary, *The Abstract of Principles* was an additional statement of faith.)

Now, after 153 years of satisfactory reliance on *The Baptist Faith and Message* as a guideline (beginning in 1925, with minor revisions in 1963), fundamentalists have made two quick revisions to it (1998 and 2000). Should current teachers who were contracted to teach under the 1963 guidelines be forced to comply with the 1998 and now the 2000 revisions? It would seem unethical, if not illegal, to breech a contract and require such compliance. While new teachers employed after the revisions were made could legitimately fall under the new guidelines, those already contracted should be "grandfathered" and allowed to continue under *BFM1963*.

(2) Should teachers be forced to affirm the adopted doctrinal statement "as a matter of conscience" or instead, as in the past, should they be asked "to teach in accordance with the statement"?

Traditionally, SBC seminary faculty members were expected to "teach in accordance with and not contrary to the statement of faith." This language was used intentionally instead of more restrictive words requiring teachers to "endorse the statement as their personal belief and commitment." The latter wording would, of course, make the faith statement a creed, violating individual conscience.

As it was under the original wording, professors might have certain disagreements with the statement, but they could agree nevertheless to teach in accordance with it. Of course, if the gap between a teacher's conscience and the adopted faith statement became so great that the teacher could not in good faith and honesty continue to teach in accordance with the statement, then the teacher would be expected to leave, or disciplinary action could be taken.

Al Mohler recently shifted from the historical position at Southern Seminary and now requires his teachers to "hold these convictions as personal beliefs and commitments, not merely as contractual obligations for teaching."[15] Even some who acknowledge the right of seminaries to expect a professor's teaching to comply with the institution's faith statement, believe Mohler's approach moves into serious creedalism.

Ken Hemphill's recent message on Southwestern Seminary's web page appears to be contradictory. He stated, "The revised *Baptist Faith and Message* is not being forced on anyone," but then he declared it would be required of all faculty at the seminary.

In summary, some Baptists believe these changes in *BFM2000* signal a clear drift toward making the denominational statement of faith an enforced creed—contrary to a long history of Baptist refusal to elevate any man-made creed above the Scriptures. Traditional Baptists are not so much "non-creedal" as they are "one-creedal"—honoring no creed but the Bible.

4. The diminishing of the doctrine of the autonomy and freedom of the local church under the leadership of the Holy Spirit.

Other critics see in the *BFM2000* an apparent weakening of the historic conviction that each local Baptist congregation is autonomous under the leadership of the Holy Spirit, and is therefore free from denominational control. From their beginning, Baptists have resisted any kind of hierarchy, any form of "top-down" governance mandating official decrees from a central denominational office. They have fiercely defended the right of each congregation to make its own decisions as they believe God leads them—even if others think they are wrong.

This does not mean that a local church can believe anything and still have the right to participate in Baptist associations or conventions. Baptist conventions and associations are also autonomous, and messengers can, and do, set limits and criteria for participation. But *BFM2000* signals a trend toward more authoritarian control over local congregations.

As an example of this trend, critics point out that, along with the other deletions discussed in this chapter, revisers also deleted these words that had appeared in *BFM1963*:

"The church is an autonomous body." In place of a separate declaration of the principle of autonomy, one word was inserted in the first sentence of the existing article on the church, giving it what critics believe is a less important emphasis: "A New Testament church of the Lord Jesus is an autonomous local congregation."

Of concern also is the prohibition in *BFM2000* limiting whom a local church can call as pastor. This is a direct intervention in the church's freedom to choose its own leaders, another violation of local church autonomy. This issue is discussed further in "troubling factor" number 8.

5. The trend toward "five-point" Calvinism and an attendant mistrust of personal Christian experience.

There are features in *BFM2000* that some believe give, for the first time, a distinct Calvinistic slant to the statement. Since Al Mohler, a leading shaper of *BFM2000*, claims to be a Calvinist, it is easy to suspect that some of the changes have more to do with Calvinistic theology than Baptist history. It appears to be an effort to redirect SBC theology toward what Mohler calls "the Calvinism of the original founders of Southern Seminary"—in contrast to the more balanced position of later Baptist theologians, such as E. Y. Mullins and W. T. Conner.

When Al Mohler was asked in a Texas meeting in September 2000 if he were a "five-point Calvinist," he replied, "I will fly my colors boldly. If you ask me if I'm a Calvinist, I'm going to have to answer yes, but that is not the first, second, third, or even fourth term I would use." He continued by explaining that his beliefs are better described as "in the Reformed tradition."

> Every Christian, every Baptist has to believe in predestination. There's not a person in this room who doesn't believe in limited atonement—as opposed to universalism. . . . The difference is in how it is limited.

In the same meeting, Paige Patterson admitted that he and Mohler hold opposing views on the doctrines of election and predestination and that he finds no biblical basis for the Calvinist opinion Mohler embraces.

> However, Calvinists strongly affirm the authority of the Bible, and that's a greater point of agreement than the two points of disagreement. . . . I'd rather have Dr. Mohler hanging around my seminary than someone who had doubts about the Scriptures.[16]

One further evidence of this Calvinist tone is the apparent mistrust of personal experience expressed in several of the revisions of *BFM2000*. These include the removal of Jesus as the criterion of interpretation, diminishing of soul competency and priesthood of the believer, greater emphasis on creedalism, weakening of local autonomy, and narrower expression of God's foreknowledge.

Strict Calvinism minimizes individual Christian experience. It prefers to think of the essence of Christianity as an acceptance of a set of unrevisable doctrinal propositions rather than a direct experience of grace or an encounter with the living Christ. In a conference at Southern Seminary in February 2001, Al Mohler attempted to simplify the divisions in the SBC by characterizing the two opposing camps as the "truth party" versus the "liberty party." He believes that the first party (his party) emphasizes the authority and inerrancy of Scripture while the second (those who opposed the takeover) emphasizes personal experience. His analysis echoes the Calvinistic preference for doctrinal propositions and its mistrust of personal Christian experience.

Mohler's Calvinist convictions shed further light on his disparaging of E. Y. Mullins's emphasis on Christian experience. Mohler blames Mullins's view for contributing to the "present state of theological 'anemia' among Southern Baptists:

> Mullins set the stage for doctrinal ambiguity and theological minimalism. He
> was near the liberals in his approach.[17]

To suggest that E. Y. Mullins was a liberal who put personal Christian experience above the biblical authority, or that he made experience the central organizing principle of his theology, is either to seriously misread or to intentionally distort Mullins's view. While rightly giving great importance to each believer's personal encounter with Christ as a powerful apologetic tool, and while identifying a personal relationship with the living Christ rather than a list of propositional truths as the essence of faith, Mullins made it clear that personal experience must always be judged by the authority of the Bible. He said Christian experience must never be used to test the Scriptures. The experience of the Christian can at best only confirm them. He wrote:

> Experience would ever go astray without the ever-present corrective influence
> of the Scriptures, but the authority of the Scriptures would never become for
> us a vital and transforming reality apart from the working of God's redeeming
> grace among us.[18]

This Calvinistic mistrust of experience may have been one motive for revising *BFM1963*. They wanted to minimize—if not reject—the emphasis on soul competency and the priesthood of the believer in *BFM2000*.

A second evidence of a Calvinist drift is the inclusion for the first time in an SBC statement of faith a stricter definition of God's foreknowledge. Also, in the section on God, the revisers of *BFM2000* added:

> God is all-powerful and all knowing; and His perfect knowledge extends to all things, past, present, and future, including the future decisions of His free creatures.

Also, in the subsection on God the Father, the revised statement adds, "all knowing" to the other attributes.

Many, probably most, Baptists believe God could control everything and everybody, but instead He chooses to be in charge rather than in control of everything all the time as strict Calvinists propose. The Bible teaches that while God is all knowing, He often chooses to limit Himself in His relationship with the world. The SBC has historically drawn from the best of both Calvinist and Arminian theology, benefiting from a continuing dialogue between proponents of both views. But these new additions tend to shut down any healthy theological discussion of God's knowledge and human free will by an arbitrary vote of the convention. This led the editor of *Christianity Today* to warn:

> Historically, orthodox Christians—Catholics and Protestants, Arminians and Calvinists—have affirmed God's complete knowledge of all future events. More recently, however, some theologians have advocated an openness-of-God theology that claims God's knowledge of the future is limited. The new SBC confession affirms that God's "perfect knowledge extends to all things, past, present, and future, including the future decisions of his free creatures." . . . Shutting down the debate by convention fiat runs a serious risk. Though openness theism clearly runs counter to historic Christian theology, it draws on certain aspects of the biblical witness that not all mainstream theologians have integrated into their teaching. The ongoing debate gives these teachers a chance to make their theology more fully biblical while remaining true to the tradition.[20]

Many Baptists believe a confession of faith is more useful if it deals with central core doctrines, leaving believers free to differ over secondary details. Our doctrinal discussions are more useful when we follow the dictum, "In essentials, unity; in non-essentials, liberty; in all things, charity."

6. The trend shifting Baptist identity from its Anabaptist, Free Church tradition to a reformed evangelical identity.

Some see the general tone of the document's changes as a watering down of historic Baptist distinctives in order to join the circle of evangelical reformed theologians, "embracing their schools, and promoting their books." In order to join the circle, Baptists have to de-emphasize such beliefs as the individual soul's direct access to God, freedom from political or religious coercion in all matters of faith, a free church in a free state, and the supremacy of Scripture over all creeds, councils, confessions, conventions, or religious authorities.[21]

This shift obscures the rich heritage Baptists draw from their English Separatists, Anabaptist, and Free Church roots and link it instead with the American evangelical movement. Unlike Baptists, the evangelical churches often "claim descent from one of the Protestant reformers, require adherence to a particular creed, or worst of all, seek political power to establish their church as a national church. This is not the Baptist way."[22]

Further reasons for this concern are the changes in statements about the Bible, which more clearly align the SBC with the view set forth in the evangelical "Chicago Statement on Inerrancy." Also cited in the Winter 1999 edition of the school's theological journal as evidence of this drift toward an evangelical identity is its defense by Southern Seminary staff member Sean Michael Lucas: "it is time to return to the founders of the SBC trained in the hardy doctrinal tradition of the Princeton Theology."

7. The narrow interpretation of the role of women in marriage.

Revisers included in *BFM2000* the earlier amendment on the family adopted by the SBC in 1998. This amendment has aroused strong criticism focused mainly on two concerns.

The first is balance. The newly added statement on the family is longer and more detailed than the sections on God, Jesus Christ, the Holy Spirit, or the Scriptures. The *Baptist Faith and Message* is intended to be a simple, condensed summary of core biblical doctrines, leaving individuals free to apply and draw out the significance of these basic truths into more specific applications as cultural changes require. In the view of some, the new article is an overstatement giving unbalanced emphasis to one area above others of greater significance.

The second criticism is that the amendment, which includes the statement, "A wife is to submit herself graciously to the servant leadership of her husband," is based on deficient biblical interpretation, adding some words not in the Scriptures, and selectively omitting other biblical teachings on the same subject. For example, the amendment does not make clear that the primary passage used to justify a wife's submission (Ephesians 5:21-33) begins with the statement "Submit yourselves to one another." Furthermore, while they refer to the husband's responsibility to love his wife, they do not explain that the word for "love" (agape) means an unselfish submission to another. Properly understood, then, the Ephesians passage also calls for equal, if not greater submission of husband to wife.

As it stands, the revision is a faulty, one-sided expression of male authority in marriage that is not biblical. It seems to be another rendering of the hierarchical pattern (God—> man—> woman—> child) popularized in the 1970s and 1980s by groups such as Bill Gothard's "Basic Youth Conflict Seminars."

8. The narrow interpretation of the role of women in the church.

BFM2000 introduces a more restrictive view of the role of women in the church. In section VI on The Church, after weakening the statement on local church autonomy, the revision adds, "While both men and women are gifted for service in the church, the office of pastor is limited to men as qualified by Scripture."

This is the first time a Southern Baptist statement of faith has expressed such a restrictive interpretation of the Scriptures—an interpretation on which Baptists have always felt free to differ.

Defending the new statement, the committee claims:

> The Bible is clear in presenting the office of pastor as restricted to men. There is no biblical precedent for a woman in the pastorate, and the Bible teaches that women should not teach in authority over men.[24]

Paige Patterson dismissed those who disagree with the committee's revision by saying, "The problem is they have to argue with God, not with us." Such language gives the impression that those who framed *BFM2000* have the only orthodox interpretation of the biblical passages. It arrogantly dismisses the viewpoints of other equally conservative, equally pious interpreters who have an equally high view of the authority of the Bible.

For example, other conservative interpreters believe the passage in 1 Timothy 1:8-15, which is usually translated, "I permit no woman to teach or to have authority over men; she is to keep silent," is not prohibiting all women from teaching men, but is merely a warning that a wife should not publicly correct her husband in the worship service of the church. They believe the passage is intended to protect the marriage relationship, not to limit a woman's leadership role in the church.

Similarly, in 1 Corinthians 14:34, "The women should keep silence in the churches," the word "keep silence" used here means "keep silent in this one instance." In verse 30, the same word is used for men who are to keep silent when another is speaking. Some conservatives believe the passage means wives are not to interrupt or correct their husbands publicly in church. This is another instance of Paul's desire to preserve the marriage relationship, not restrict women from participating in worship leadership.

After all, in 1 Corinthians 11:2-9, Paul acknowledges that women are to "pray and prophesy" in church. When they do, they should wear proper apparel and appropriate hairstyles. Surely these alternate conservative interpretations should not be condemned but be humbly acknowledged as possibilities.

A recent article in *Christianity Today* reminds the revisers of *BFM1963* that denominations like The Church of the Nazarene, Church of God, Evangelical Friends, Free Methodists, The Salvation Army, and The Wesleyan Church all are considered theological conservatives who take their Bibles seriously, but they all share a long heritage of women pastors and preachers.[25] They base their view on what they consider to be a careful exegesis of the Scriptures. The article further points out that conservative television teacher James Dobson is happy to claim that his grandmother was the "primary pastor" of a local church. Dobson's *Focus on the Family* allows women ministers.

Contrary to some defenders of *BFM2000*, there is no clear statement in the Scriptures prohibiting women from serving in any church leadership position. Therefore, in the light of these differing conservative interpretations, the authors of *BFM2000* should in all humility admit that while they prefer their interpretation, it is not the only legitimate view. Other conservative, evangelical, biblical positions on the role of women in the church should be equally permissible.

An editor of *Christianity Today*, after acknowledging that the view expressed in *BFM2000* restricting the role of women in the church is in line with Greek Orthodox and Roman Catholic doctrines of the priesthood, warns:

> Elevating this matter to the level of confessional status seems to us an unnecessary departure from the historic Baptist traditions: no previous Baptist confession has spoken to this matter directly. . . . Clearly some SBC critics fear that the revised statement will become a litmus test. "Instead of building a consensus statement, they are using it as a club to drive out people they disagree with," one SBC leader said.[26]

Curiously, no parallel prohibition was included in *BFM2000* against the ordination of women to be deacons, although the New Testament names the diaconate along with the pastorate as an office of the local church.

9. The "Pandora's Box" concern: a fear of repeated future revisions to include favorite opinions.

Another source of dismay about *BFM2000* has been labeled the "Pandora's box" concern. Those who believe *BFM1963* did not need to change, worry about the recent trend of ever more frequent revisions, tightening up the confession of faith every few years by adding details. Believing "Pandora's Box" has been opened, they wonder, "What's next?" "When?"

In the past, traditional Baptists have allowed and even encouraged diversity of opinions on secondary theological issues not considered core biblical doctrines. Within the broad parameters of *BFM1963*, pastors, teachers, theologians, lay and denominational leaders, led by the Spirit, were free to hold varied interpretations on such issues as women in ministry, Calvinism, worship styles, millennial views, and the nature of biblical inerrancy. This confession of faith has served the Baptist family satisfactorily by a broad consensus until 1998 and 2000. Surely any changes in a proven document that has served us so well for so long would be only rarely and reluctantly considered.

According to one evangelical writer, confessions serve better when they focus more strongly on the central affirmations of the Christian faith, the faith once delivered to the saints. Confessions not only err by being too loosely constructed, they also err by being too tightly drawn. We must remember we are called to preserve the peace and unity of the church as well as its purity.[27]

In 1826, Kentucky Baptist leader S. M. Noel made a similar observation about confessions:

> They should be large enough to meet the exigencies of the church by preserving her while in the wilderness, exposed to trials, in peace, purity, and loyalty. And they should be small enough to find a lodgment in the heart of the weakest lamb, sound in the faith.[28]

In a similar vein, Baptist theologian Roger Olson offers a useful analysis of theological categories. He says Christian beliefs through the years can be grouped into three levels:

(1) Dogmas–such great essential Christian convictions as the trinity, incarnation, creation, *sola scriptura*. These define the essence of Christian belief and are worthy of serious and heated defense.

(2) Doctrines–denominational distinctives, such as immersion of believers, once saved always saved, congregational church government. These are crucial, but those who hold them would not denounce those who don't as non-Christians.

(3) Opinions–such as details of events surrounding the second coming of Christ, worship styles, the exact nature of angels, and dates for creation. One might also include in this

level some features of Calvinism and various views about women in ministry. Baptists have always allowed differences in this area of opinions. (Protestant reformers labeled this category *adiaphora*, from a Latin term for "things that don't matter very much.") Olson suggests that denominations get in trouble when they try to elevate "opinions" to the level of doctrine or dogma.[29]

Given the legalistic tendency of ultra-conservatives to impose narrow doctrinal interpretations, some fear there is a danger, even a likelihood, that other hard-line opinions will soon be added as future SBC committees keep tinkering with the statement. One can understand the anxiety on the part of Bible-believing conservative teachers whose careers are in the hands of powerful and often unpredictable hard-liners. Remember, one of the new SBC leaders who had a major influence in revising *BFM2000* once said, "If we say 'pickles have souls,' then the seminaries must teach that 'pickles have souls.'"[30]

One can't help but wonder, what will the next round of revisions bring? This is one reason some Baptist bodies are refusing to adopt *BFM2000*, preferring to stay with *BFM1963*.

10. The false accusation of neo-orthodoxy in the content of BFM1963.

BFM2000 dropped the term "record of revelation" from Section I on the Scriptures, explaining that the term is an example of "fuzzy, neo-orthodox-sounding language" in *BFM 1963*. Neo-orthodoxy was a twentieth-century theological movement led by Karl Barth and Emil Brunner that attempted to replace liberalism with a more conservative position. It often fostered the belief that Scripture was only a "record of revealed truth" until it was read and believed. Such statements led critics to believe neo-orthodoxy did not move far enough away from liberalism. So the authors of *BFM2000* falsely assume that anyone who calls the Bible a "record" of revelation is thereby diminishing its authority. Granted, the Bible is indeed a revelation from God, but it is equally true that it is a record of God's revelation.

Those who oppose the new *BFM2000* claim that describing the Bible as a "record of revelation" helps clarify the fact that revelation first came through God's mighty acts and words in the history of Israel and through the incarnation of Jesus Christ, God's supreme revelation of Himself to humanity. The Bible shares in that revelation, but it is, first of all, an inspired record of God's revelatory acts. This is not a liberal concept, nor does it belong exclusively to the neo-orthodox movement. It is a valid evangelical and Baptist idea, and it belonged in *BFM1963*.

11. The trend toward including a catalogue of specific sins.

A confession of faith is intended to be a simple, condensed summary of core biblical doctrines, leaving individuals free to apply and draw out the significance of these basic truths into more specific applications as cultural changes require. This is why the *BFM1963* was reluctant to list specific sins to be opposed, focusing instead on general concepts such as greed, selfishness, and vice. To list, as the revised statement does, a specific catalogue of contemporary sins believers should avoid will soon solicit additional revisions from others who want their favorite sins included too. Critics of *BFM2000* see this as a weakness.

12. Inconsistency.

Finally, a relatively minor criticism is raised about inconsistencies in *BFM2000*. In their introduction and defense of the new revisions, the committee declares the need to challenge boldly a hostile culture with a new announcement of Christian convictions, yet revisers seem to have yielded to that "hostile culture" by weakening the statement on keeping the Sabbath in Section VIII, "The Lord's Day."

The strong, traditional language of *BFM1963* calls on believers to observe the sanctity of the Lord's Day by refraining from "Worldly amusements, and resting from secular employments, work of necessity and mercy only being excepted." A more "liberal" accommodating suggestion in *BFM2000* replaced those words with the following: "Activities on the Lord's Day should be commensurate with the Christian's conscience under the Lordship of Jesus Christ." This seems to contradict the pronouncement by Adrian Rogers that the revisions were needed to offset a "pervasive secularism that has infected our society."[31]

Another inconsistency is seen in the fact that their revised wording, "Christian's conscience under the Lordship of Jesus Christ," sounds very much like the freedom of individual experience under the Lordship of Jesus to which the revisers object in their removal of the Christocentric principle of hermeneutics.

Further inconsistencies are noted in the frequent references in *BFM2000* to the importance of Christian unity, peace, voluntary cooperation, and harmony while at the same time moving in a more restrictive direction that creates disharmony and division.

CONCLUSION

Southern Baptists at their best have been and always will be what John Newport called "constructive conservatives" in theology. However, it is easy for this constructive form of conservatism to degenerate into rigid extremism. Southern Baptists should heed the warning of J. I. Packer in the book *Power Religion*. This work exposes an evangelical drift into what it calls "Carnal Conservatism," whose characteristics are telling:

1. Authoritarian styles of leadership.
2. The use of secular political strategies to organize and take control.
3. Fanning emotional fears by supposed conspiracy theories.
4. Government entanglements that reduce the church to nothing more than another special interest group.
5. The use of peer pressure to enforce conformity, ganging up, ostracizing, withholding rewards from those who refuse to go along.
6. The total defeat of those who disagree (which the book calls an ugly denominational version of ethnic cleansing).

Several years ago, Al Mohler expressed similar concerns about the future of the SBC. Although he has recently been less than conciliatory both in his rewriting and defense of *BFM2000*, his earlier more conciliatory plea is worthy of consideration:

> The future shape of the Convention must avoid the twin dangers of obscurantist, angry, and separatist fundamentalism on the right and revisionist compromise on the left. In between lies the evangelical option—an irenic, bold, and convictional posture which combines concern for orthodox doctrine with a spirit of engagement with the larger world and a missionary mandate.[32]

To these words, most Baptists would say, "Amen."

NOTES

[1] W. W. Barnes, *The Southern Baptist Convention* (Nashville: Broadman Press, 1954), 118.

[2] *The Baptist Faith and Message 1925*, Preamble.

[3] *The Baptist Faith and Message 1963*, Preamble.

[4] *The Religious Herald* (25 May 2000): 8.

[5] Quoted by Roger Olson, "Theology for the Rest of Us," *Christianity Today* (22 April 2002): 68-69.

[6] *Biblical Recorder* (29 July 2000).

[7] *Associated Baptist Press* (5 June 2000).

[8] *Baptist Standard* (26 February 2001).

[9] *Christianity Today* (7 August 2000): 36.

[10] *Southern Seminary Magazine* (June 2000).

[11] *Baptist Standard* (17 July 2000).

[12] *Biblical Recorder* (29 July 2000).

[13] *Baptist Standard* (17 July 2000).

[14] Sermon, 15 July 2000.

[15] Recurring Southern Seminary advertisement in *Christianity Today*.

[16] *Baptist Standard* (12 November 2000).

[17] E. Y. Mullins, *The Axioms of Religion—Library of Baptist Classics* (Nashville: Broadman & Holman Press, 1997).

[18] E. Y. Mullins, *The Christian Religion in its Doctrinal Expression* (Philadelphia: Roger Williams Press, 1917), 27.

[19] *Christianity Today* (7 August 2000): 37.

[20] *Western Recorder* (12 February 1999).

[21] Ibid.

[22] *Baptist Standard* Internet report, 11 November 2000, 2.

[23] *Christianity Today* (4 September 2000): 105.

[24] *Christianity Today* (7 August 2000).

[25] Ibid.

[26] Ibid.

[27] Roger Olson, *The Story of Christian Theology* (Downers Grove IL: Intervarsity Press, 1999), 17.

[28] *Fort Worth Star Telegram* (October 1998).

[29] Adrian Rogers, BCE critique on internet newsletter (10 May 2000).

[30] *Christianity Today* (7 August 2000).

A WICKED AND PERVERSE GENERATION DEMANDS A SIGN(ATURE)

BY KENNETH MASSEY

When you file an income tax return, you are required to sign it. When you write an personal check, you put an official signature on that piece of paper. Every time you use a credit or debit card, your "autograph" is required. Legal documents require signatures.

I've been signing my name on paper as long as I can remember. I've signed up for classes, and in those classes I have been required to put my name on tests and assignments. I've put my "John Henry" on job applications. True love wasn't enough for a marriage license. The County Clerk required me to sign on the dotted line (which I would do again in a heartbeat, my love).

Signing our names has become such a routine, we repeat it without concern and treat it as mundane rather than meaningful. Signatures, however, are more than official inscriptions. Names are personal representations of who we are. Like fingerprints, they are unique vehicles that embody something basic about our nature or essence.

It goes back to the biblical notion. Names are more than verbal or written designations. "To know the name of a person was to know that person's total character and nature."[1] We are commanded to honor and respect God's name because the divine name and the divine nature are inseparable.

Signatures today have been reduced to legal and functional "seals of approval." Signing has become more about identification than identity or integrity. The biblical importance of our names, and how we use them, is all but lost.

Alas, this consecrated concept is being remembered and reclaimed. All we needed was a crisis, and the International Mission Board (IMB) of the Southern Baptist Convention (SBC) has offered us one.

The IMB has decided that missionaries must sign the 2000 *Baptist Faith and Message* (*BFM2000*). Other SBC agencies and institutions also require this of employees. On a legal and institutional level, signing obligates IMB missionaries to teach and work within the doctrinal parameters of the confession.

On a more subtle and spiritual level, however, requiring their names on a manmade document of faith binds their "character and nature" to these human principalities and powers, not to God or Scripture. It does not matter who writes the creed or what it says, Baptists refuse to be bound to anything or anyone other than Christ.

IMB missionary Stan Lee has expressed this very well in a letter that has been widely distributed. He writes, ". . . to pledge to any other document outside God's Holy Word violates my beliefs as a Baptist and my integrity before God."[2]

This missionary, serving in Rwanda, East Africa, believes he is being pressured to sign a statement of beliefs by "small-minded contentious little men whispering lies in the hallways and back rooms of power in the SBC." He compares these men to those who despised Daniel (Dan 3:8-12).[3] Dr. Lee also likens forced signing of *BFM2000* to the idolatry imposed by King Nebuchadnezzar when he decreed that everyone bow before his golden image. This is one Baptist missionary who cannot submit his name to anyone other than his Lord.

What's in a name? More than meets the eye. What do leaders want when they demand our names? They want for their own a lordship reserved for the One God. Why will some refuse to sacrifice their names on the altars of creed and conformity? Because their names have been written freely in the Lamb's Book of Life, and that is enough.

WHAT'S IN A NAME?

Growing up Baptist, I was taught that followers of Jesus do not "lord it over" other members of their spiritual family (Matt 20:25-27). My teachers warned me of people and denominations that "exercise authority" over servants of Christ. I was taught to respect and submit to the authority of Jesus and Scripture.

I share these concerns as a Baptist pastor who has served four congregations in three states. I've served blue-collar and white-collar Baptists, suburban, rural and urban Baptists, formally educated and self-educated Baptists, pious and earthy Baptists, wealthy and poor Baptists, visceral and intellectual Baptists, Sandy Creek and Charleston Baptists, and that list doesn't narrow it down much.

I am currently serving First Baptist Church in Greensboro, North Carolina, a traditional, generous, missionary Baptist congregation. At this time, we give most of our mission money through the Cooperative Baptist Fellowship (CBF) and our Baptist State Convention. Nevertheless, we still pray for and support IMB missionaries.

At this writing, our church had just completed a two-week medical/dental/construction trip to Chile, sending thirty-eight volunteers to work with IMB personnel. We have done these trips for several years because we have an historic relationship with Baptist work in Chile. We have no ill will for Southern Baptist missions or missionaries. To the contrary, we want the best for these servants of God.

If you totaled all Cooperative Program (CP) gifts by our congregation since 1925, I believe our church would be among the top ten churches in total CP giving. For many of those years, we gave fifty percent of all receipts to the CP and led North Carolina in giving to missions. This congregation has an historic and sizeable investment in Southern Baptist missions and missionaries.

I wish my love for Southern Baptist missionaries could be expressed in glowing affirmation and sacrificial support for the IMB. That is not possible. I must discover another way to be faithful to missions—a way that is fruitful and true, even if difficult and painful.

I find myself groping for a way, and the search leads me to an old Baptist barn. It is in that dark and musty place, filled with cobwebs and memories, that I find it. It's rusty, but strong. Better hands than mine have held it and used it. Some have been punished for doing so.

As I take it from its resting place, an old nail in a pegboard, it feels heavy and my heart quickens. Can I use this? Will it work? Yet there is something familiar to its feel, like an old friend of the family you've never met. This is what I will use in my quest to be a free and faithful lover of missions and missionaries. It is called *Dissent*.

A CASE FOR DISSENT

Keepers of orthodoxy, emboldened by the synergy of their own righteousness, always disregard or destroy dissenters as heretics. Our beloved Baptist forebears didn't relish the role, but neither did they shrink from it. Their dissent was demanded by their consciences, not by their inclination toward discord. Baptists don't need more discord, but neither do we need the dogma that is being forced upon our missionaries, agencies, local churches, associations, and related state conventions.

I could begin by offering a critique of revisions made to the *Baptist Faith and Message* in 1998 and 2000, but others, including Russell Dilday in this volume, make that case very well. Instead, my focus will be on how *BFM2000* is being used as a tool for purging, coercing, and controlling Southern Baptists, especially missionaries.

Before I speak about this anathema, let me state that I do not presume to know or judge the hearts of those who crafted the new confession, nor do I claim to be superior to any of them as a Christian or theologian. I refuse to judge another person's servant. I will not try to score points on them by comparing them to terrorists or infidels.

I am writing out of my own attempt to remove the plank from my eye. In that process, I have come to the conclusion that coerced confessions provide more splinters than light to our eyes.

Leaders of the SBC have spoken and written about their goals, and I understand these to be among them:

1. Less "wiggle-room" in Southern Baptist doctrine generally and the *BFM* specifically;
2. More clearly defined parameters of belief and practice in Southern Baptist institutions and churches;
3. Clearer and more historic lines of distinction between male and female roles in family and church;
4. Resisting or turning back the tide of cultural decline/pluralism in America.

Of course, SBC leaders have other goals, many of them noteworthy, I'm sure. This is not a critique of every facet of Southern Baptist life. It is a warning about the new Southern Baptist quest for doctrinal purity.

Whatever ails us, theologically, institutionally, or relationally, will not be healed or helped by requiring signatures on the *BFM2000*. That document is a statement of faith written by a handful and affirmed by less than one-tenth of one percent of Southern Baptists (those present and voting at the convention).

WHERE WILL THIS ROAD OF MANDATORY BELIEF LEAD SOUTHERN BAPTISTS?

Through Scripture and story, I will suggest that this road of priestly power will lead Baptists to places we don't want to go. It will lead to (1) denominational authority, (2) pseudo-security, (3) purgative purity, (4) dubious discipleship, and (5) unfaith.

Denominational Authority

SBC leaders will say they are pursuing and promoting authentic biblical authority. While I affirm the Baptist notion of scriptural authority, I reject the idea that any denomination, convention, agency, or oligarchy can become the keeper of that authority, or be the locus of that authority. The Keys belong in local churches.

In the book of Revelation, we can read seven letters to seven historical local churches. The first of these is written to a congregation in Ephesus, the foremost city of Asia Minor. Ephesus was a religious center known for its magical arts. It was home of the Mother Goddess, Artemis, and her temple. Ephesus became a center for worship of the Roman Emperor.[4]

It was in Ephesus that Paul spoke against Artemis and a riot ensued. It was here that Paul labored in the church and was loved by the church. Acts 20 reports a tender scene as Paul bids farewell to the elders of the church in Ephesus. After he had told them they would never see him again, *he knelt down with all of them and prayed. They all wept as they embraced him and kissed him. What grieved them most was his statement that they would never see his face again . . .* (Acts 20:36-38).

Jesus says to his church in Ephesus, *I know your works, your toil and your patient endurance. I know that you cannot tolerate evildoers; you have tested those who claim to be apostles but are not, and have found them to be false* (Rev 2:2).

This strategic church is commended because the people are willing to undertake the difficult work of spiritual discernment. This church believes, with the apostle James, that *faith without works is dead* (James 2:14-26). They have been taught that *a tree is known by its fruit*—by what it produces (Matt 7:16; Luke 6:43). The Ephesian church is committed to truth and righteousness.

The church *cannot tolerate evildoers*. Her work of discernment takes place within the congregation. She is not commended for hating and attacking evil outside the church. She is not weeding sin out of the world. Rather, she is determined to deal with falsehood and abusive authority in her own ranks.

The evildoers in Ephesus have a name: Nicolaitans. We know little about them other than what we read in Revelation. They are making false claims about apostolic authority, claiming they have it. They are "self-styled apostles who claimed a position over that of the local elders."[5]

Baptists, like Ephesians, do not tolerate "self-styled" apostles who claim authority over local congregations. We may not be discerning about all things, but we've been committed to that principle since day one.

This chapter does not speak to any specific doctrinal deficiency among the Nicolaitans. For all we know, there was nothing "false" about their belief, per se. They are "false" because of their works and because of the authority they claim over the leadership of the local church (Rev 2:6).

The Ephesian church is not commended because she weeded out every questionable belief. She is commended for her backbone. She will not cave in to those who claim a greater authority than Jesus and his teachings. She can tell the difference between sheep and wolves in sheep's clothing.

Local congregations today have access to the same spirit (Spirit) of discernment. We need no confession or creed claiming doctrinal or ethical authority over us. We need twenty-first-century Nicolaitans even less. This essential and often neglected work of discernment belongs to local congregations. It's not just the Baptist way. It's the biblical way.

For the record, I believe the local church should promote sound doctrine and should, within its own ranks, be intolerant of false teaching and immoral living. This difficult work, however, is not the righteous realm of denominations, bureaucrats, or conventions. Discernment is our job in the local church, even if we fall short in the effort. It is better to work for spiritual integrity and fail than to surrender responsibility to overlords and dominions. When doctrinal and ethical oversight becomes the domain of denominations, we wind up with an ecclesiastical KGB.

There is another warning in this text. The good work of moral discernment is no substitute for love. Ask any wife if a hard-working husband is an acceptable substitute for a loving husband, and you'll get the same answer.

In our efforts to resist the authoritarianism of modern Nicolaitans, we can forsake our first love. Discerning spirits can become critical spirits. God help us! No matter what we do for our Lord or how passionately we do it, without love, it will amount to nothing (1 Cor 13).

The church in Ephesus is told to do two things. *Remember then from what you have fallen* (Rev 2:5). Can local congregations remember that we take our cues from the Spirit, not from denominational principalities and powers? Can we remember that Scripture is our authority and not anyone's commentary on it (including mine)?

The church is also told to *repent*. Christ tells the church to *do the works you did at first* (v. 5). What a huge distraction this doctrinal and denominational purging has been—not only to churches, but also now to missionaries.

The challenge to remember and repent is followed by a troublesome warning. Jesus says, *I will come to you and remove your lampstand from is place, unless you repent.* I believe God will judge congregations that forsake love. He will remove them from their places of service and influence. He will use others to accomplish his purposes. This may be true of conventions and mission agencies as well.

Pseudo-Security

John is a man who inherited a beautiful Victorian house from his grandfather. After a legal dispute over the estate and estrangement from his father and older sister, John decided to make that house his home.

Moving from the city to the Central Plains had been a dream, even though the area was located in tornado alley. John was glad to get away from the chaos of the city and eager to make improvements to the grand old home place.

The first thing John planned for his new house was an expansive basement. Why would anyone in tornado alley not have the security of a basement? In addition to security, a lower level is warmer in winter and cooler during those dog days of summer.

One of John's nephews, an engineer, warned him about underground water in the area. He thought a fan, a back porch, and a cellar for the tornado warnings would be a better alternative. John would not be deterred from his decision to dig.

It wasn't easy finding a contractor willing to add a basement under a seventy-five-year-old house. He found someone with an impressive education and a larger ego to get the job done.

This engineer did all he could to secure the structure of the home in the process, but even before the basement was finished, doors were getting stuck and windows wouldn't open. Cracks appeared in and around the house. John always patched them quickly. He didn't want the "little lady" to be alarmed.

When water began seeping into the excavation under the house, John seemed to become more and more determined to have that basement. He studied and planned as much as the engineer and decided to sell a few acres to pay for the installation of french drains and sump pumps. He had the basement walls sealed with a tar-like material that was supposed to be impenetrable.

The finished product was quite impressive—roomy and furnished. John reminded his neighbors that it was quite an engineering feat. With a half smile bordering on a smirk, John invited them all to return next time they heard the tornado siren blaring.

John's personal sense of vindication was as thrilling to him as the new space. He had known all along what was best. He tried to be humble, but it was difficult. When the first tornado warning sounded, the entire family retreated into the safe and comfortable basement, knowing they were beyond the reach of the whirlwind. It was just what John had wanted.

Soon, however, dark patches began to appear, first in the lower back corners of the basement, but quickly spreading to other areas. John's wife made valiant attempts to fight the encroaching growth, but it kept reappearing. The children began having allergic reactions and stopped going downstairs. John could not accept that unfriendly *fungi* were plaguing his new basement. When he finally tore out the sheet rock, he was horrified to see the dark green growth literally filling the walls of his beloved basement.

John wanted a secure and efficient living space for his family when he built that basement. What he ended up with, after five years of fighting, was a glorified mold farm under a sagging old house. The city inspector recently left a green tag on the door.[6]

Frequently, when we work to get something we want, we discover that we have also earned something we didn't want in the process.

Southern Baptist leaders know what they want for the SBC and her institutions and agencies. They have been focused on that goal for years. They want to make the denomination more secure from the whirlwind of cultural chaos.

The *BFM2000* is their "basement." This new Baptist "foundation"—this new underbelly of the old house—will give them, and many other Baptists, what they want. It really will. Tragically, the mandatory *BFM* will also give Baptists what we don't want.

Making allegiance to *BFM2000* the primary litmus test for being Southern Baptist will create more doctrinal uniformity among cooperating state conventions and churches. It will "unburden" the convention of partners in ministry who aren't completely loyal and committed to the conservative resurgence. This strategy might even enlarge the denomination as formerly independent churches join the SBC fold. It might even make Southern Baptists feel more secure . . . for a time.

Such security and prosperity are a mirage. *BFM2000* is a Hollywood set. Walk down the street and you think you're in the 1950s again. You can imagine a *Leave It To Beaver* world, but it's only an illusion. If every Southern Baptist on the planet signed *BFM2000*, they would not be immune to cultural influence, doctrinal diversion, or old-fashioned moral failure.

On top of that, even if pledging allegiance to this human creed could grant us security, what would it undermine in the process? Jesus uses a better image to address the question.

You are familiar with the parable of the wineskins in Matthew, chapter 9. Jesus says that if you put new wine into old wineskins, the old wineskins will burst, the wine will be wasted, and the wineskins ruined (v. 17). Instead, you put new wine into new wineskins.

There are two distinct Greek terms used in this parable, both of which are translated *new*. One means *new in time* and the other means *new in quality or nature*.[7] The latter term is used of the new wineskin. New (fresh) wineskins are forms, rituals, and ways of life into which Jesus can and will pour his life and love.[8]

Jesus is confronting a religious establishment that is zealous to keep everyone and everything within its righteous boundaries. He is giving warning about a religious way of life that is too rigid and inflexible for his use. These old straightjacket systems of sacred security lock in a certain kind of uniformity and conformity, but in the process they also lock out the new wine of the Spirit.

That's the trouble with old wineskins like creedalism and legalism. They quench the Spirit. They become substitutes for living and growing faith. They confuse the relative value of wine and wineskin, with an unhealthy emphasis on the latter.

Authentic Christian conversion (sanctification) requires wineskins that will stretch because new life in Christ is a growing and dynamic process. Static faith is dying faith, even if it is wrapped in sound doctrine. The writer of Hebrews warns us to *move beyond the elementary teachings of Christ and go on to maturity* (6:1). He does not say move beyond error to truth or beyond poor doctrine to right doctrine. He simply calls us to let our beliefs grow and enlarge in fresh wineskins. Followers of Jesus cannot mature if the pulp of their living faith becomes petrified or putrefied.

BFM2000 may be new in time, but it is old and brittle in quality. It is an old wineskin of religious power and control. Its framers declare that it was written to remove "the wiggle room" from the 1963 version. The new *Baptist Faith and Message* is designed to be more rigid and inflexible than its predecessors.

This theological tower of Babel is so right and tight, even the Spirit won't find room to move or stretch. Whenever we lock up our beliefs (right or wrong) in a rigid system of man-made propositions, we hinder the Spirit from moving and stretching us to deeper truth.

Does this mean there is no absolute truth? I say "No!" It means there is no absolute human understanding. It means human interpretation is always incomplete. It means we never live up to or completely understand divine absolutes.

I think the authors and promoters of *BFM2000* believe they are protecting the faith and preserving sound doctrine. I share many of their concerns about theological entropy. Creating an inflexible wineskin of denominational accountability, however, is not the solution. No confession or creed will ever hold the new wine of God's Spirit.

Purgative Purity

Once again, we turn to a story by Jesus. The parable of the tares is placed after the famous parable of the sower in Matthew 13.

You know the story line. The kingdom is like a man who sows good seed in his field, but an enemy sows weeds in the same field. The owner's servants discover this after the wheat and weeds have been growing together for some time. They discover it when the fruit of each becomes visible.

The servants have a solution. They offer to "take care of the weeds." They will put them in cement overshoes. They will make them wish they had never been sown. They will rip them up one weed at a time, if necessary. Breaking their thumbs won't do. Tradition names these servants Lefty and Guido.

They believe the owner has planted only good seed. They know the owner does not want to harvest weeds. They know the owner wants a bountiful harvest of wheat. They are only trying to give their master a pure and worthy field.

And how does the owner reply to the suggestion? No. Do not pull up the weeds, he says, *because while you are pulling the weeds, you may root up the wheat with them. Let both grow together until the harvest. At that time I will tell the harvesters: First collect the weeds and tie them in bundles to be burned, then gather the wheat and bring it into my barn* (Matt 13:29-30).

The master may fear that wheat and weeds are growing so close together that roots are entangled and one will not come up without the other. The other concern might be that servants, as well intended as they may be, are not infallible in their discernment. Even good servants can mistake wheat for weeds. Better to let them be.

However you may interpret the meaning of the parable, it is clear that the weeds represent the work and product of the Evil One. Some biblical interpreters have understood the weeds as people. Others have understood them to represent whatever is contrary to the righteousness of God.

Clearly, servants of God do not have the right to root out evil, heresy, immorality, etc. Christians do not have the authority to rid the world of that which they believe is contrary to the will of God. We may not like it, but the weeds of this world get the benefit of sunshine and rain . . . just like the wheat. Only God may separate wheat and weeds, and that will happen at harvest time.

For me, the parable is told to help the servants of Jesus live faithfully in a world that is an unpleasant mixture of good and evil. This undesirable mix extends to the four corners of the earth and to the private corners of my heart. The parable shows us the difference between God's work and our own.

The parable of the net (Matt 13:47-50) presents a similar picture. The kingdom net sweeps through the water of the world catching all manner of creatures, good and bad, large and small, crappie and carp. Fishers do not pick and choose which fish will be caught or which creatures will be pulled on board the boat.

The kingdom net is "no respecter of persons." The angels of God, at the end of the age, will separate the righteous and the wicked. This is *not* the responsibility of those who do not own the boat, who merely hold the net. No one in Baptist life has the authority to expel the wicked from the redemptive hand of God.

I have managed to get my hands on the new "textual fragment," *circa* 1960s, that Southern Baptist "archaeologists" have "discovered." These manuscripts include an extended ending to the parable of the weeds. This expansion will be included in the new *Never To Be Revised Again Bible* coming to a LifeWay store near you. The fragment seems to pick up after v. 30.

Two of the servants met in a quiet inn to discuss the disaster that had taken place in the owner's field. "I don't like what I see," said the first.

"Neither do I," echoed the second.

"Weeds everywhere you look. There isn't a section unaffected."

"I know the master is heartbroken about this flagrant act of deviance."

"What are we going to do? Part of me wants to plow the whole field under."

"The master said do nothing. He said we should wait until the harvest."

"You don't think he really meant that, do you?"

"I found it difficult to swallow. This is our way of life. Those are our fields in a way."

"That's the point. We are closer to the field than the master. He sowed the seed, but we see that field every day. I don't think the master knows how many tares have been sown among his wheat."

"I'm not sure he realizes the damage they can do while we just sit here doing nothing. Didn't he warn us about weeds that choke the very life out of his seedlings?"

"Maybe he meant, let them grow together unless we see that the wheat is being damaged by the weeds. Surely he would want us to step in if that were the case."

"I had another thought. He may have meant that restriction for the women. They really don't know farming like we do. Some would probably be confused between wheat and weed. He was probably saying that so they wouldn't make a mess of things. I think I could rid us of the problem without hurting the wheat."

"I've been praying about that, too. The master is away, and I don't know when he'll be back. We'll have to make a decision, and I think the master would want us to do what's best for his crop."

"What do you propose?"

"Let's not say this to the entire group. Let's get a few good friends together who really see the problem like we do. Let's start in one corner and by the time everyone sees what we have done, we'll be able to show them our trophies."

"Yes, a burning pile of weeds and a pure, undefiled section of field. They will have to go along."

"What if we accidentally damage some of the wheat?"

"I've thought of that. We'll just replace it. It's not that difficult, especially when you have a field of dreams."

"One more thing. How are we going to make sure we get all the weeds? Some of the servants don't have our eyes."

"We'll give them a battle cry and tell them the master's plantation depends upon their work. We'll remind them that weeds come from hell. How about this to rally the troops: 'If in doubt, pull 'em out.'"

"We should be rewarded appropriately."

All of us see the conflict in Baptist life through different lenses. I see the doctrinal purge through the frame of this parabolic ending that seems to mirror the birth of the SBC "takeover" strategy in a New Orleans café in the 1960s. I believe untold harm has been done to the Master's harvest because some of his servants cannot abide living in a field where everyone is not as righteous or orthodox as they are. The SBC doesn't seem to want a net that sweeps up diverse people and their unacceptable ideas.

Even if Southern Baptist leaders know the difference between orthodoxy and neo-orthodoxy, they must leave judgment to God. Even if they have allergic reactions to weeds, they cannot extract them. Even if they feel the Master's pain because they think people are twisting the truth and disobeying the commandments, they may not assume the role of their Master.

A good systems theorist might conclude that SBC leaders are chronically anxious. Anxious people often project their failure onto others. Anxious systems often react to pain by purging scapegoats.[9]

Peter Steinke writes:

With little capacity for discernment, the chronically anxious reduce everything to all or nothing. Lines are drawn. It is no wonder, then, that they overfocus on others and their weaknesses. They blame and falsely criticize.[10]

. . . Blaming is a sign that people are stuck in their instinctive nature. The blame game resembles an ancient religious practiced called "divination"— locating the source of evil (which is believed to be outside of oneself) and eliminating it.[11]

Steinke goes on to compare the self-destructiveness of anxious systems to a failure of the body's healthy immune system. When I read this, I see *BFM2000*:

Many diseases—multiple sclerosis, rheumatoid arthritis, allergy—are the result of the immune system gone berserk. They are called autoimmune diseases. Somehow or other the white cells begin to attack living tissue as though it were a harmful intruder. The white cells call on the forces of expulsion. Every explosive device at their disposal is turned on simultaneously and exuberantly. When a "usually healthy reaction turns cannibalistic," physician Paul Brand notes, "a dreadful civil war" commences in the body. In the hostile presence of these defensive cells, there is overkill. More damage occurs to the host than to the invader. The defense becomes the disease. What is designed for self-protection becomes destructive.[12]

The International Mission Board's defense has become the disease. The conservative reaction in the SBC looks like "reptilian regression." This attack on living members of the Baptist family by self-appointed "white cells" is a sign of an "immune system gone berserk." It's a sorry method of atonement.

None of us has been commissioned to judge another man's servant, but that's what *BFM2000* does in the hands of purgative priests. This denominational weedeater will become a disastrous wheatwhacker.

I know of a case in Scripture where a person was "weeded out" from congregational fellowship because of sinful behavior, not poor doctrine (1 Cor 5). In that chapter, Paul warns us that church discipline is only appropriate in the context of the local assembly. Any other attempt at judgment and expulsion, condemnation or coercion is outside the calling of God (1 Cor 5:12-13).

Another biblical example of Paul's refusal to punish and purge because of doctrine or conviction is found in Romans 14. Even though a ruling about not eating meat sacrificed to idols was delivered to the churches by the Jerusalem Council (Acts 15:29), Paul was not bound by this "authoritative proclamation." He stood for the freedom of personal conviction and refused to be bound by the decision of the Council.

In that 14th chapter of Romans, Paul also tells us not to put a stumbling block in our brother's way (v. 13). Forcing signatures on *BFM2000* has *stumbling block* written all over it.

Dubious Discipleship

BFM2000 is coming your way. Like an intravenous injection, this potent blend of religion and politics will coarse through every vein in the Baptist body. Some congregations, state conventions, and associations will use it just like the IMB is using it. No matter how much we claim local church autonomy, we have trouble standing against this kind of collective pressure.

I have encouraged the church I serve to resist this creedal version of being Baptist for these reasons:

1. It undermines authentic Bible study. The study of Scripture has always been a core Baptist discipline. At our best, we gather in small groups to tackle the teachings of Scripture and gather the courage to live them out.

Bible study groups are like juries. They consider the biblical evidence together. They attempt to reach a "verdict" about how this evidence should be understood and obeyed. At times, they may see it differently and reach diverse conclusions. At other times, they may reach consensus.

When denominations codify the truly important theological tenets, however, they leave only doctrinal leftovers for those of us who study the Bible in our churches. The SBC is saying to us, "You can read about women in the Bible if you want to, but we have already issued the last word on that subject."

You cannot learn math by looking at the answers in the back of the book. We cannot truly engage Holy Scripture without the freedom to disagree. We learn through the process of struggle and failure. This author knows no other way for Scripture to become personal belief and practice.

Bible study, at its best, is like eating. Scriptural truth must be bitten off, chewed, swallowed, and digested. *BFM2000* is a doctrinal drip—a feeding tube for those who are deathly ill and dependent on white-robed priests.

BFM2000 will not produce a healthy denomination or vital mission force because it undermines spiritual growth through honest and prayerful inquiry into "the whole council of God."

2. It undermines authentic accountability. SBC leaders have created for us, in *BFM2000*, a self-styled "instrument of doctrinal accountability." We already have one, thank you very much. It is the local church with an open Bible and freedom to follow Christ. That's the New Testament plan of Christian accountability.

Mutual submission, out of reverence to Christ, is our way of life (Eph 5:21). We exercise watchfulness over each other. If a church member is caught in sin, other brothers and sisters intervene to restore that friend. The work is always guided by grace and love and is always reciprocal (Gal 6:1-5).

This kind of biblical accountability flourishes in communities of trust and intimacy, not in huge centralized organizations. I am not opposed to spiritual accountability and church discipline. I'm opposed to my denomination, state convention, or association acting as the *Alpha* and the *Omega*—the beginning and the end—of that accountability.

Congregations who pledge their ultimate loyalty to the SBC and its creed will be content to submit to convention leaders. That is not a Baptist way to be accountable.

Unfaith

Why must Southern Baptist leaders take biblical interpretation into their own hands? Why must there be a doctrinal purge by denominational leaders? Why must we enable a spirit of suspicion and criticism about those who serve Christ as our missionaries?

SBC leaders have their own explanations, but I would suggest one that is more fundamental (Yes, I can use the word, with no"ism" or "ist" on the end). Current SBC leaders send a definite message that they do not have any measure of trust in local Baptist congregations. You don't grab the steering wheel away from the person who is driving unless that person has lost control of the car. SBC leaders are saying (actually, they are screaming), "You can't be trusted with Scripture alone!"

They are grabbing the wheel from local churches because they do not believe we can get our theology right. Evidently, they believe the job of biblical interpretation has become too difficult for congregations. Not having the zeal and discernment we used to have, we must need "Big Brother Baptist" to look over our shoulders.

The great irony about how *BFM2000* is being used is this: Those who defended the *inspiration* of Scripture are now dismissing the *illumination* of the Spirit. From those who claim "the highest" view of the Spirit's work in creating Scripture, we get "the lowest" view of the Spirit's ongoing work of guiding the believer into truth.

Like golfers clearing a course when lightning strikes, I believe thoughtful Baptists are going to stay far away from that which undermines and underestimates the work of the Holy Spirit. I'm clearing out of any movement, statement, or denomination that acts as though the Spirit needs our help rather than the other way around. It sounds too much like blasphemy.

Jesus said to the Sadducees, *You are mistaken, not understanding the Scriptures or the power of God* (Matt 22:29).

I don't know the source of this story about Bob and Barb, two commuters who knew each other only by sight. They rode the same train every day. Both lived in Connecticut, but worked in New York. One day, anxious to get home and running late, they hopped on the train just before it pulled out of the station.

Bob saw one empty seat and rushed to get it before an elderly woman could make her way to it. He laughed to himself as the woman tried to maintain her balance in the moving train. Barb saw what happened and graciously offered her seat to the stooped-over woman.

The young girl sitting next to Bob had lost her purse. Timidly, she asked him if she could have a quarter to call home when she arrived at the train station. "No way," Bob said. "Get a job." Barb slipped a quarter into the hand of the young girl and gave her a smile.

There was a *No Smoking* sign in the car, but Bob decided he deserved a smoke. He lit up a cigar, filling the car with a light blue haze and a pungent odor. Barb opened her window to let in some fresh air.

If I asked you to identify the *good* person and the *bad* person in this story, you would have no trouble. Even all Baptists might agree about who was right and who was wrong. Ours would not, however, be a New Testament answer.

Bob and Barb were both wrong. In their stress and confusion at the end of the day, they boarded the wrong train. No matter how right you are, a train going to Albany will never get you to Connecticut.

BFM2000 is the wrong train. No matter how good or how bad its theology, it will take us away from freedom in Christ. No train of denominational domination will ever take us to "the city that is to come," but only to some deserted dead end depot.

It doesn't matter who writes it or who enforces it, local congregations don't need a creed, when the Word made flesh is leading us home.

NOTES

[1] Kandy Queen-Sutherland, "Naming," in *Holman Bible Dictionary* (Nashville: Holman Bible Publishers, 1991), 1006-1007.

[2] This is a powerful letter, written by a missionary who chooses integrity over expediency. See Stan R. Lee, "A Statement of Faith," *Texas Baptists Committed* (April 2002): 25.

[3] Ibid., 26.

[4] George Eldon Ladd, *A Commentary on the Revelation of John* (Grand Rapids: William B. Eerdmans Publishing Co., 1972), 36-41.

[5] Robert H. Mounce, *The Book of Revelation* (Grand Rapids: William B. Eerdmans Publishing Co., 1977), 87.

[6] Inspired by the actual exploits of an unwise neighbor and a nasty basement in a former church building.

[7] W. E. Vine, *Expository Dictionary of New Testament Words*, vol. 3 (Old Tappan NJ: Fleming H. Revell Co., 1940), 109-10.

[8] "General Articles, Matthew-Mark," in *The Broadman Bible Commentary*, vol. 8, ed. Clifton J. Allen (Nashville: Broadman Press, 1969), 130.

[9] Peter L. Steinke, *How Your Church Family Works* (Bethesda MD: The Alban Institute, 1993).

[10] Ibid., 21.

[11] Ibid., 54.

[12] Ibid., 107-108.

HISTORIC BAPTISTS DENOUNCE CREEDALISM

BY CHARLES W. DEWEESE

Freedom, cooperation, and accountability constitute a dynamic trio of ideals throughout Baptist history. Each has brought much to the table of congregational and denominational achievements. Success has hinged, however, on proper balance among these three principles. Today, imbalance prevails; accountability dominates freedom and cooperation.

When the Southern Baptist Convention (SBC) termed the 2000 edition of the *Baptist Faith and Message* (*BFM2000*) an "instrument of doctrinal accountability," it applied a blowtorch to the foundational Baptist principle that God has gifted each individual in every church, association, convention, and mission field with liberty of conscience. No inside or outside authority has any right—at any time or place—to force beliefs on any Baptist (including SBC agency employees). The Baptist responsibility is to teach disciples and nurture missionaries, not to cripple their soul competency and intelligence with binding statements intended to subjugate them. Trust is more biblical than control.

The SBC imploded between 1979 and the early 2000s for at least six reasons: (1) It told its heritage of freedom to get lost; (2) It elected officers, trustees, and CEOs committed to jugular-cutting ethics; (3) It rewrote its history to support a control agenda; (4) It raised pastoral authority to unconscionable levels; (5) It demeaned women in ministry and laity in general; (6) It turned creedal—mocking academic freedom in its own seminaries, denying basic rights of belief to its own missionaries, and questioning the rights of its constituents to think for themselves. This chapter will focus on creedalism, particularly its background.

Yes, the SBC still has agencies, money, and buildings. But serious illness has afflicted its heart, soul, and spirit. The non-Baptist public senses it. Thinking Baptists know it. Put simply, the SBC decided that it would create rules for belief and punish all who broke them. That stance is producing two guaranteed results: liberty-loving Baptists who treasure nonconformity refuse to submit; and SBC integrity is dying a slow death.

The SBC Executive Committee is the most powerful body in SBC life. Through recommendations of that committee, the SBC has locked itself into a mode of creedal intimidation and power that defies the best judgment of 400 years of Baptist history and ideals. Monthly articles in *SBC Life*, published by that committee, verify it. In tentacle-like fashion, creedal thrusts from the committee have tightened the doctrinal screws on theological education and missions, distorted curriculum literature, slammed women in ministry, hurt Christian witness, and defamed the Baptist image. Put simply, the SBC has made creedalism the centerpiece of its "Baptist reformation" trophy case. Creedal application of written confessions of faith has become normative.

Morris H. Chapman, president and CEO of the Executive Committee, told that body in his February 18, 2002, presidential report that "we are a people who believe not in a creed, but in a confession."[1] Tell that to the hundreds of professors, missionaries, and denominational employees of SBC agencies who have forcibly lost jobs or resigned in defiance over harsh creedal applications of the 1963, 1998, and 2000 editions of the *Baptist Faith and Message*. These people can prove that creedalism is alive and well in the center of SBC life today. In fact, it is the whip that SBC leadership systematically uses to create pain for all who resist. Today, many missionaries are justifiably crying out against such abuse.

"Jesus is Lord" is a classic example of a New Testament confession of faith. It is intensely personal, voluntary, and meaningful. From the first utterance, its non-coerced depth and simplicity served as a freedom-based model for all future Christians. Throughout his earthly ministry, Jesus promoted relationship-based faith and combated rigid, legalistic, and punitive uses of doctrine. Creedalism is forced faith. At Jesus' death, God forever made nonsense of creedalism by tearing the temple curtain into two parts.

Every Baptist is responsible only to God in matters of conscience—not to the state, not to the church, not to pastors, not to seminary presidents, not to mission board executives, and especially not to creedal statements. God must surely take offense when denominational leaders circumvent liberty of conscience by trying to force specific doctrinal views on other people's lives.

Baptist news is saturated with discussions about confessions and creeds. In recent times, Associated Baptist Press, Baptist Press, Baptist state newspapers, *Baptists Today*, Cooperative Baptist Fellowship and Mainstream Baptist publications, major city newspapers, Baptist websites, and other news outlets have published articles that address issues related to these matters. Misuses of confessions always cause Baptists to cry "foul."

The SBC established itself in the 1800s and 1900s as one of the most successful missions-delivery denominations in world Protestantism. That reputation faces extreme risk. A large issue is the relationship between missions and confessions of faith. Historically, voluntarism has driven both. Today, voluntarism drives neither. Treated as a creed and forced on missionaries, on theological faculties who train missionaries, and on curriculum literature that prepares students to consider mission opportunities, the *BFM2000*, in its application, turns voluntarism into legalistic compliance. People, faith, missions, and Baptist principles suffer painfully in the process. Yes, missionaries continue to volunteer to serve—but, agonizingly, they discover that their mission-board employers require them to abandon all sense of freedom in what they believe.

In 1988 W. Morgan Patterson, president of Georgetown College and an excellent Baptist historian, presented a list of dangers about which Southern Baptists needed to be cautious. One danger implied a significant connection between inordinate focus on doctrinal requirements and the ministry needs of the world. Patterson cautioned "that, in our concern for doctrinal orthodoxy in every detail, we may forget the spiritual needs of multitudes of people who need the gospel of Christ."[2]

Baptists emerged into world history in 1609. Immediately, they began to create and print confessions of faith. That practice continues today. Individuals, churches, associations, conventions, and other Baptist organizations have drawn up and adopted confessions. Through such statements of belief, they simply confess their basic doctrinal views. Although most Baptists have freely used and defended confessions, not all have. The Separate Baptists of the 1700s, for example, raised concerns about using them, fearing creedal applications.

Baptists have attempted to construct confessions upon the teachings of the Bible. Because existing confessions vary dramatically in their emphases, Baptists have obviously interpreted Scripture in diverse ways—thereby reflecting strong appreciation for four Baptist ideals: soul competency, the priesthood of all believers, the right of private interpretation of Scripture, and the role of autonomy in Baptist life.

Across the centuries, Baptists have inserted a heavy dose of voluntarism into the adoption of confessions. Typically, they have claimed that an approved confession applies only to the specific individuals or groups who adopt it, whether those persons are in congregations, associational meetings, convention gatherings, or other denominational settings. Ideally, such confessions affect no one other than the individuals who subscribe to them.

Often, churches and other Baptist bodies have assumed that confessional statements represent the common beliefs of *all* their constituents. This in itself has violated the intent of confessions. Those beliefs could not possibly represent the views of all the other Baptists who did not vote on them, even if they were in the same church or other body, especially in view of Baptists' insistence that the Bible is the sole written authority for their faith. Admittedly, an organization can vote to give a confession doctrinal authority, but then it is no longer a confession; it is a creed.

Confessions can be useful. They can serve as guides to Bible study. They can identify the principles that characterize a group of Christians. They can distinguish one group of Christians from another. They can identify common denominators between groups of Christians. Confessions can illustrate the valuable role of voluntarism in the Baptist experience.

However, dual allegiance to the Bible and confessions of faith has promoted inevitable conflict of interest for Baptists for almost 400 years. Only one of the two can be officially, completely, and finally authoritative. That is the Scripture. Confessions are secondary, derivative, non-canonical. They are not the final word. Nevertheless, Baptists, at times, have relied far more on confessions than on the content of the Bible in defining who they are.

One dynamic principle has governed the historic Baptist approach to confessions: they are not creeds. Granted, at times in their history some Baptists have loosely used the word creed as synonymous with confessions. However, a creed implies mandatory authority; it presumes legalistic compliance; it assumes the form of regulatory law; it demands uniformity and subjugation to the will of the body; and it involves forceful application and negative effect for refusal to submit.

Creedalism contradicts nonconformity, and nonconformity lies in the center of the Baptist soul. Creedalism negates freedom, and freedom is the driving force of the Baptist spirit. Creedalism derives from the desire to control, and Baptists resist efforts to impose belief. Creedalism presumes that a church, association, or convention has the right to dictate to individual Baptists what and how they should believe, and Jesus taught his disciples to think for themselves. Jesus never exalted personal confessions into creeds applicable to others.

Converting free belief into an enforced creed results in a mindless uniformity of conviction for those who cave in to such pressure. For readers who think this could never happen to Baptists, perhaps a couple of reminders will help.

For one thing, a recent claim by one of the top Baptist historians in America can quickly snap us back into reality. H. Leon McBeth asserted in 1987 in his comprehensive textbook on Baptist history that the *Baptist Faith and Message* adopted in 1963 by the Southern Baptist Convention "has become more creedal than any other [confession of faith] in Baptist history."[3]

Further, the 1987 SBC-adopted Peace Committee Report prescribed an extremely narrow, four-point interpretation of the *Baptist Faith and Message* article on the Bible. And the 1998 and 2000 revisions of the *Baptist Faith and Message* have defined even more narrowly such matters as the submission of women to their husbands and exclusion of women pastors, and it has removed Christ as the criterion for interpreting the Bible.

Baptists have attempted to exhibit balance in the doctrinal emphases presented in their confessions. But confessional imbalances flourish today, particularly at the key points of downgrading the role of Jesus as the criterion by which to interpret the Bible, suppressing women in marriage and ministry, and injecting such oppression into the hiring practices and continued employment of denominational agency personnel.

Veteran missionaries of the SBC International Mission Board (IMB) began being victimized by this imbalance in 2002, when the IMB asked them to sign the *BFM2000*. That was already being required of newly appointed IMB missionaries. When the SBC assigns inordinate authority to a confession, that process becomes a denominational albatross—a liability to Baptist success.

Evidence abounds that some contemporary Baptists thrive on twisting confessions into creeds, thereby violating the historic Baptist ideal of voluntary belief. Therefore, this chapter will exhibit indisputable, plain-as-day, historic Baptist objections to converting voluntary confessions into nonvoluntary creeds.

Unlimited evidence could be produced, but three selected types of resources will suffice: (1) what confessions say about themselves; (2) assessments of creedalism by scholars who have studied confessions and Baptist history extensively; and (3) a lecture series at a major Baptist university. Writings and writers will be allowed to speak for themselves in quotable quotes.

1. CONFESSIONS OF FAITH SPEAK FOR THEMSELVES

What do historic Baptist confessions themselves say or imply about how they should be used? Thomas Helwys set the pace in 1611 as writer of the first English Baptist confession. Helwys had the help and consent of laypersons in his small congregation in preparing the confession. Article 10 stated that the church consisted of faithful people separated from the world by God's word and Spirit and knit unto the Lord and one another by baptism upon their own confession of the faith (citing Acts 8:37) and sins (citing Matt 3:6).[4]

These two Scripture verses present verbal, voluntary confessions of faith by individuals in the context of believer's baptism. They confessed their sins and declared belief in Jesus Christ as the Son of God. Nothing else mattered.

The 1644 *London Confession*, which had a major shaping influence on Baptist life, stated significantly in Article VII: "The Rule of this knowledge, Faith, and Obedience, concerning the worship and service of God, and all other duties, is not mans inventions, opinions, devices, lawes, constitutions, or traditions unwritten whatsoever, but onely the word of God contained in the Canonicall Scriptures."[5] This claim represented a powerful caution against making any documents or oral traditions equivalent with the Bible; that, of course, included confessions.

The 1654 confession of London Baptists titled *The True Gospel-Faith*, noted for being the first Baptist confession calling for the laying on of hands on all baptized believers, included an introductory letter. That letter compared the authority of confessions to the authority of the Bible. Confessions lost. Note the exact wording:

> We therefore do desire that whosoever read it [the confession] may weigh the Scriptures produced; and if it be according to the Scriptures, there is light in it; for it's the Scriptures of the Prophets and Apostles that we square our faith and practice by, accounting that light within (not witnessed by the Scriptures without) which some so much talk of to be deep darkness. . . . Let the Scripture therefore be the rule of thy faith and practice. . . .[6]

This internal assessment of this confession shredded all possibility that it could be applied in a creedal fashion; in fact, it denied that it could even be used as a confession if it departed from Scripture.

The *Second London Confession* of 1677 and 1688, featuring a pronounced Calvinism, served as the basis for the 1742 *Philadelphia Confession* that dominated Baptist life in America in the eighteenth century. Sentence one of Chapter I of the *Second London Confession* obliterated the notion of using confessions creedally by claiming that "the Holy Scripture is the only sufficient, certain, and infallible rule of all saving Knowledge, Faith, and Obedience. . . ." And Chapter XXI dealt another blow to creedalism:

> God alone is Lord of the Conscience, and hath left it free from the Doctrines and Commandments of men which are in any thing contrary to his word, or not contained in it. So that to Believe such Doctrines, or obey such Commands out of Conscience, is to betray true liberty of Conscience; and the requiring of an implicit Faith, and absolute and blind Obedience, is to destroy Liberty of Conscience, and reason also.[7]

Significantly, the 1925, 1963, and 2000 editions of the *Baptist Faith and Message* adapted the thought of Chapter XXI in these words: "God alone is Lord of the conscience, and He has left it free from the doctrines and commandments of men which are contrary to His Word or not contained in it."

Thus, the *Second London Confession* and the *Philadelphia Confession* undercut creedalism with two powerful principles: (1) biblical authority and (2) freedom of conscience.

The 1833 *New Hampshire Confession* referred to the Bible as "the supreme standard by which all human conduct, creeds, and opinions should be tried."[8] The 1925, 1963, and 2000 editions of the *Baptist Faith and Message* used those exact words with one exception: each inserted the word "religious" prior to the word "opinions." As a prominent doctrinal statement of nineteenth-century Baptists, the *New Hampshire Confession* reinforced in the Baptist mind the absolute necessity of framing all doctrinal development around the teachings of Scripture. That precluded the imposition of creedal statements on anyone.

At the 1925 SBC meeting in Memphis, Tennessee, E. Y. Mullins, renowned Southern theologian and president of the Southern Baptist Theological Seminary, presented the report of the Committee of Baptist Faith and Message. That report recommended the adoption of the SBC's first confession of faith, and it was adopted. Because the committee was apprehensive about how the confession might be used, it included a preface that provided unambiguous guidelines for approaching confessions:

> Baptists approve and circulate confessions of faith with the following understandings, namely:

That they constitute a consensus of opinion of some Baptist body, large or small, for the general instruction and guidance of our own people and others concerning those articles of the Christian faith which are most surely held among us. They are not intended to add anything to the simple conditions of salvation revealed in the New Testament, viz., repentance towards God and faith in Jesus Christ as Saviour and Lord.

That we do not regard them as complete statements of our faith, having any quality of finality or infallibility. As in the past so in the future Baptists should hold themselves free to revise their statements of faith as may seem to them wise and expedient at any time.

That any group of Baptists, large or small, have the inherent right to draw up for themselves and publish to the world a confession of their faith whenever they may think it advisable to do so.

That the sole authority for faith and practice among Baptists is the Scriptures of the Old and New Testaments. Confessions are only guides in interpretation, having no authority over the conscience.

That they are statements of religious convictions, drawn from the Scriptures, and are not to be used to hamper freedom of thought or investigation in other realms of life.[9]

In 1963 another Committee on Baptist Faith and Message, under the chairmanship of Herschel H. Hobbs, SBC president and pastor of the First Baptist Church of Oklahoma City, presented for adoption a revised edition of the 1925 statement, and the SBC adopted it. The revised statements retained the five points included in the 1925 preface.

The 1963 preface, however, stated even more emphatically that confessions are not to be used in creedal fashion: "Such statements have never been regarded as complete, infallible statements of faith, nor as official creeds carrying mandatory authority." It asserted that "the sole authority for faith and practice among Baptists is Jesus Christ whose will is revealed in the Holy Scriptures." And it claimed that "Baptists emphasize the soul's competency before God, freedom in religion, and the priesthood of the believer."[10]

In 2000, the SBC adopted a revised edition of the *Baptist Faith and Message* contained in a *Baptist Faith and Message* Study Committee Report. This committee was chaired by Adrian Rogers, pastor of the Bellevue Baptist Church in Cordova, Tennessee, and former SBC president. The 2000 edition repeated exactly the five-point statement included in the prefaces to the 1925 and 1963 editions. It reaffirmed the "principles of soul competency and the priesthood of believers." (For the record, the committee's original report deleted these historic emphases; the committee reinserted them after much protest from conservative Southern Baptists.)

Ironically, the 2000 preface included one new element that explicitly laid out how the SBC tended to use the confession. It described confessions as "instruments of doctrinal accountability." Rather than being voluntary statements of faith, now they were "instruments" (tools, weapons, agents of force). Rather than being means of expressing personal or community faith, now they were techniques of "accountability" (authoritative, demeaning, compliance-oriented). Although Article I described the Bible as "the supreme standard by which all human conduct, creeds, and religious opinions should be tried," in practice the SBC does precisely the opposite; the *BFM2000* takes priority over the Bible in determining the acceptability of professors, missionaries, and other denominational personnel.[11]

The SBC mindset of applying confessions creedally closely matches the approach of some fundamentalist Baptists of the 1940s. In 1921 the fundamentalist Fellowship of the Northern Baptist Convention adopted a confession by Frank M. Goodchild whose preamble opened with the following sentence: "The adoption of a creed to which allegiance is demanded would be contrary to our historic Baptist principles and repugnant to our deepest spiritual instincts."[12]

Then in 1943 the fundamentalist Fellowship organized the Conservative Baptist Foreign Mission Society. That society adopted the Goodchild confession but deleted Goodchild's preamble, including his statement about creeds, and, in its place, inserted the following:

> Only those persons who, without reservation, fully and freely subscribe to the following doctrinal statement are eligible to vote, and only those who without reservation will subscribe to [it] by signing the following doctrinal statement annually are eligible to serve as officers, regular employees, or missionary representatives of the society.[13]

Do elements of that approach sound familiar in SBC life today?

Of course, they do. Fundamentalism, in any era, is a system of religion that thrives on doctrinal domination. Its corporate insecurity about freedom drives its desire to control thought. In sharp contrast, Jesus never tried to control anyone's doctrine. He encouraged discipleship, not oppression.

Baptists have resisted creedalism on a worldwide basis. Confessions of Baptists in other countries have also countered creedal possibilities, particularly by stressing the sole written authority of the Bible. The 1879 confession of the Union of the Baptist Churches in France designated the Holy Scriptures as "the touch-stone for testing every tradition, every doctrine, and every religious system."[14]

A 1908 confession of German Baptists (revised from one adopted in 1848) claimed in Article 1 that the Bible "must be the sole rule and plumb-line of faith and practice" and in Article 10 that "the unchangeable rule and plumb-line of the church remains the New Testament."[15]

A confession drawn up from 1974 to 1977 was adopted by German-speaking Baptists in Austria, the Federal Republic of Germany, the German Democratic Republic, and Switzerland. The preamble made an extremely important point: "This confession of faith is an expression of and a witness to the churches' agreement of belief. Thus it cannot itself be an object of faith or a compulsory law for faith. As a summary interpretation of Holy Scripture it is grounded in and limited by Scripture."[16]

2. SCHOLARLY ASSESSMENTS OF CONFESSIONS AND CREEDALISM

Four key books, one in the 1800s and three in the 1900s, printed the texts of major Baptist confessions, presented their histories, and commented on them. (1) In 1854 The Hanserd Knollys Society of English Baptists sponsored the formative work *Confessions of Faith, and Other Public Documents, Illustrative of the History of the Baptist Churches of England in the 17th Century*, edited by Edward Bean Underhill, joint secretary of the Baptist Missionary Society. (2) In 1911 the American Baptist Publication Society published *Baptist Confessions of Faith* by W. J. McGlothlin, professor of church history at the Southern Baptist Theological Seminary. (3) In 1959 (rev. 1969) Judson Press published *Baptist Confessions of Faith* by William L. Lumpkin, pastor of the Freemason Street Baptist Church in Norfolk, Virginia. (4) In 1982 Broadman Press published *Baptists in Europe: History & Confessions of Faith* by G. Keith Parker, then a faculty member at the Baptist Theological Seminary in Ruschlikon, Switzerland.

These four respectable scholars expressed common opinions about vital confessional issues.

Underhill cut the freedom trail:

> The confessions of this volume were not creeds, compulsorily imposed on the members or churches of the Baptist body. Speaking strictly, they were apologies, taking the form of confessions . . . as the most convenient way of informing adversaries of the matter of their faith. No one was required or bound to subscribe to them, and if adopted by any church as the expression of its sentiments, all others were left free, and even a considerable latitude of judgment allowed in the bosom of the church itself. . . . They were not framed to procure unity among the churches that accepted them. They sought to reflect the existing sentiment, and the scriptural orthodoxy of the communities whose pastors signed them; they left the phantom of uniformity to the unavailing search of an establishment.[17]

McGlothlin wrote plainly:

> Being congregational and democratic in church government, Baptists have
> naturally been very free in making, changing, and using Confessions. There
> has never been among them [Baptists] any ecclesiastical authority which could
> impose a Confession upon their churches or other bodies. Their Confessions
> are, strictly speaking, statements of what a certain group of Baptists, large or
> small, did believe at a given time, rather than a creed which any Baptist must
> believe at all times in order to hold ecclesiastical position or be considered a
> Baptist. In the latter sense there has been no Baptist creed.[18]

McGlothlin then asserted the following:

> No Baptist individual, church, Association, or larger body has ever felt perma-
> nently bound by any Confession of Faith in its original, historical, or any
> other form. And yet the Baptists have preserved a remarkable degree of doctri-
> nal agreement throughout their history. This is no doubt due to their
> insistence upon a converted church-membership, the authority of the
> Scriptures, and the right and duty of every individual Christian to decide doc-
> trinal questions for himself by a study of the Scriptures under the guidance of
> the Holy Spirit.[19]

Lumpkin expressed it this way:

> Baptists have freely made, used, and discarded confessions of faith, which have
> appeared in the name of individuals, of single churches, and of groups of
> churches or denominations. For them confessions have ever been simply man-
> ifestos of prevailing doctrine in particular groups. No confession has ever
> permanently bound individuals, churches, associations, conventions, or
> unions among Baptists. Even when issued, the confessions have allowed for
> individual interpretation and perspective, so that each signatory was made to
> feel that the statements spoke for him.[20]

(In 1958 Lumpkin wrote the article on Baptist confessions for the *Encyclopedia of
Southern Baptists*. His first sentence reads: "Few Christian groups have confessed their faith
so freely as Baptists, but no group has been more reluctant than they to elevate these confessions into authoritative symbols or creeds.")[21]

Parker observed:

> There is . . . a general resistance to a creedal understanding of confessions in
> Europe. This can be appreciated in light of so many cases of large church-state

domination and a history of persecution under a creedal definition of who a Christian is and what one is entitled to believe. Due to either painful experiences or a unique history, some unions refuse to have a confession for fear it may be abused, as creeds were.[22]

Listen further to some astute comments from the foreword to Parker's book written by Penrose St. Amant, senior professor of church history at the Southern Baptist Theological Seminary:

> Baptists reject the conception of a coercive Christianity which in the past characterized the European state churches, two components of which were infant baptism and normative creeds. This condition explains the resistance of Baptists to formulating theological statements that are normative and, therefore, their insistence that such statements should be called *confessions*, which are not normative.[23]

St. Amant continued by making point-blank clear that

> no confession of faith can be an object of faith or a law demanding certain beliefs. Baptists believe that doctrinal questions should be decided in the light of the Scriptures under the guidance of the Holy Spirit. Confessions are useful because they provide theological guidelines adopted by Baptist bodies in relation to specific historical contexts and periods and are, therefore, indexes to the unity and diversity, the similarities and dissimilarities, in Baptist belief and practice.[24]

Southern Seminary's collective, long-term heritage of opposing creedalism stayed on target for many years before Al Mohler, the current president, took over in 1993. McGlothlin, Lumpkin, and St. Amant all have served as professors of church history there, and Parker earned a doctorate in church history there.

James E. Carter possesses superb understandings of Baptist confessionalism. He completed a doctoral dissertation at Southwestern Baptist Theological Seminary in 1964 on "The Southern Baptist Convention and Confessions of Faith, 1845–1945." Later, he prepared many articles and other writings on the subject.

In 1976 he wrote:

> The trail of Baptist history is littered with confessions of faith that have been adopted by various Baptist bodies then discarded, revised, or ignored. A noncreedal people, Baptists have nevertheless adopted many confessions of faith.

These confessions of faith, however, have not been authoritative statements of faith erected as official bases of organization or tests of orthodoxy.

Further, "A Baptist confession of faith does not have binding authority. It is a consensus of the belief of the body which issued the statement." In fact, "Baptists have always been careful to draw the distinction between a confession and a creed.[25]

In a pamphlet written for the SBC Historical Commission in 1979, Carter added:

> A Baptist confession of faith, sometimes called a statement of faith, is not a creed. A creed implies authority and finality, two implications which Baptists resist. Baptists have never understood their confessions to have ultimate authority; these are not the beliefs that anyone must hold in order to be a Baptist. Neither have Baptists ever considered any of their statements to be the final word on any matter of Christian faith or practice. Baptists do not desire the authority to prescribe what other people must believe or to force their beliefs on them. The strains of individual freedom and congregational church government run too deeply in Baptist life to allow that to happen.[26]

The *Review and Expositor*, journal of the Southern Baptist Theological Seminary, included eight articles in its Winter 1979 issue themed "Baptist Confessions of Faith." Many of those articles questioned the senselessness of using confessions creedally. Excerpts from two, both written by professors of church history at Southern, typify most of the others.

In his article on "Confessions or Creeds in Early Christian Tradition," E. Glenn Hinson acknowledged the values of confessions in early church history but then concluded: "The long history of misuses of confessions to distinguish orthodoxy from heresy explains the fear and even revulsion which many groups have for them. Better not to have confessions than to have persecution on account of them."[27]

Bill J. Leonard's article, "Types of Confessional Documents Among Baptists," ended with a comment and some good questions:

> In light of recent trends . . . it is clear that many Baptist bodies are at a cross-road in interpreting and utilizing confessional statements. Are doctrines to be defined more precisely and pressed more dogmatically upon churches and church members? Is the 'unity in diversity' once so characteristic of Baptist groups, to be abandoned in favor of stricter uniformity?[28]

In 1999 William H. Brackney, then principal of McMaster Divinity College in Hamilton, Ontario, and presently a professor of religion at Baylor University, published his highly significant *Historical Dictionary of the Baptists*. The introductory paragraph to his article on confessions of faith assesses the relationship between confessions and creeds:

> Historically, Baptists have understood themselves as 'non-creedal.' By this is meant that the historic creeds of the churches are non-binding on the conscience and thus may not be used for discipline, worship, or definitional purposes. Rather, Baptists affirm liberty of conscience and prefer to interpret the Bible as guided by the Holy Spirit and the church. Confessions of faith, however, are a popular means of expressing doctrinal definition and the theological traditions of congregations, associations, and institutions. The idea of a confession of faith derives from a voluntary statement of specific beliefs.[29]

3. HOBBS LECTURESHIP IN BAPTIST FAITH AND HERITAGE

The late Herschel Hobbs had a rich Baptist background and a prophetic voice. He was pastor of First Baptist Church, Oklahoma City, 1949–1972; preacher on the former SBC Radio and Television Commission's *Baptist Hour* radio program; 1958–1976; two-term SBC president, 1961–1963; chair of the committee that drew up the 1963 *Baptist Faith and Message*; and vice president of the Baptist World Alliance, 1965–1966.

After 1950, he was Southern Baptists' most articulate and widely read spokesman for Baptist ideals. Bob R. Agee, president of Oklahoma Baptist University, claimed in 1993 that in the second half of the twentieth century, Hobbs had been "the most effective thinker among Southern Baptists" and "the consummate pastor, Bible scholar, theologian who has kept us more in touch with historic Baptist perspective than any single individual."[30]

To honor Hobbs, First Baptist Church, Oklahoma City, endowed a lectureship at Oklahoma Baptist University named after him and his wife. In 1995 Providence House Publishers published *The Fibers of Our Faith: The Herschel H. and Frances J. Hobbs Lectureship in Baptist Faith and Heritage at Oklahoma Baptist University*, Volume 1, edited by Dick Allen Rader, who was vice president for religious life and dean of the Joe L. Ingram School of Christian Service at OBU. The volume contained sixteen lectures presented in the series between 1980 and 1993.

Six lectures expressed grave concern about turning Southern Baptist confessions of faith into creeds. Hobbs himself presented three of those lectures.

In 1980 he asserted that "the storm clouds of creedalism hover over our denomination" and cautioned that "we must exercise constant vigilance in warding off the threats to religious freedom, both within our denomination and outside it, including the current drift toward creedalism." Referring to the 1963 *Baptist Faith and Message*, he wrote: "Neither is it a creed, for Baptists are not a creedal people." Hobbs emphasized the New Testament-based principles of soul competency in religion and the priesthood of all believers.[31]

In a second 1980 lecture, Hobbs focused more directly on the 1963 *Baptist Faith and Message*. He observed that the committee chosen to prepare it deliberately had retained the preamble to the 1925 edition, which stated explicit opposition to turning confessions into official creeds that carried mandatory authority. He further claimed that "our committee also was careful to protect the conscience of the individual to avoid any suggestion that this statement was creedal in nature." Hobbs concluded this lecture with a strong reminder: "We must keep in mind that the *Baptist Faith and Message* is not a creedal statement. . . And Baptists are not a creedal people."[32]

Hobbs began his third lecture, in 1987, by reiterating two Baptist essentials: the competency of the soul in religion and the priesthood of all believers. Regarding competency, he affirmed that Jesus Christ is the only mediator between God and anyone and that "every person is responsible to God for his/her faith or lack of it." Then, Hobbs continued, "out of this basic belief emerge the priesthood of every believer and the democratic polity of every Baptist segment. . . . We are held together, not by a creed, but by a common purpose in evangelism and missions."[33]

Three other lectures in the Hobbs Lectureship, all by major Baptist historians, provided additional opposition to growing patterns of creedalism in Southern Baptist life. Walter B. Shurden's 1984 lecture on the "Theological Erosion of Southern Baptist Distinctives" did not mince words. Shurden reminded his listeners that the SBC had incorporated into one of its formative documents in 1845 an aversion for all creeds but the Bible.[34] Then he opined that Southern Baptists had moved a long way from that ideal: "Since the 1960s, and increasingly since 1979, the *Baptist Faith and Message* has become a criterion for orthodoxy and a code word for doctrinal purity." To be sure, "confessionalism is eroding into creedalism among Baptists." In summary, Shurden wrote, "Southern Baptists are moving from soul competency to soul incompetency, from a non-binding confessionalism to a binding creedalism."[35]

In 1985 Robert A. Baker's lecture, "Divided We Stand," delivered one of the most devastating hits against creedalism ever offered by a Baptist church historian. Considering the fact that he had served as professor of church history at Southwestern Baptist Theological Seminary for more than forty years and that he had written an official history of the Southern Baptist Convention, his assessments are particularly noteworthy.

Baker used his lecture to identify three lessons from Southern Baptist history that speak to current controversy in Southern Baptist life. He devoted about two pages to describing the first and third of those lessons. But he dedicated about five-and-a-half pages to his second lesson: "In Baptist general bodies, *diversity is better than creedalism*. The founding fathers of our Convention specifically avoided the formation of a general convention that involved creedalism. No creed or confession of faith was appended to the constitution." However, "in the last sixty years," Baker continued, "our Convention has changed its character. . . . Let me go a step farther today and state unequivocally that our Southern Baptist Convention is already a creedal body which threatens Baptist individualism and churches at their most sensitive point: what they believe."

After citing several causes of SBC's conversion into a creedal body, Baker asked a key question: "How has this change of the Convention into a doctrine-determining body violated historic Baptist principles?" He then offered a penetrating four-point response.

First, he said, "the autonomy of thousands of Baptist churches related to the Convention has been compromised" since "any binding confession of faith adopted by our Convention will differ from the confessions of faith of many churches affiliating with the Convention."

Second, "the principle of liberty of conscience is violated" because "all minority voters, whether fundamentalist or conservative or otherwise, are penultimately denied representation on the trustees of our convention agencies *because of their doctrinal views.*"

Third, "the doctrinal politicizing and creedal debates which have characterized all of our recent annual sessions of the Convention are often unbaptistic and always dangerously polarizing." In fact, "creedal uniformitarianism must always bring the danger of political intimidation." Further, "additional schisms would erupt in any newly organized creedal Convention."

Fourth,

> the creedal preoccupation of our Convention is displayed in the methodical purging of the trustees of the agencies of our Convention on the basis of creedal orthodoxy. Such doctrinal discrimination impugns the integrity of the thousands of loyal Baptists who have been vigilant to preserve scriptural orthodoxy as they have served as trustees of our Convention's agencies.

In conclusion, Baker affirmed that "a creedalistic convention is unbaptistic and unscriptural. Baptist diversity and Baptist liberty of conscience will always undermine it."[36]

In 1990, Slayden A. Yarbrough presented the sixth Hobbs lecture that zeroed in on creedalism. As Dickinson Professor of Religion at OBU, Yarbrough described the nature of doctrinal statements:

> Our confessions of faith are not creeds, they are not absolutes, they are not infallible nor eternal, they are not to be used as litmus tests for orthodoxy. They are positive doctrinal statements, expressed freely by Baptists to instruct and give guidance. . . . They are subject to revision and change, or they can be discarded at any time by Baptists who have written or subscribed to them. To use them otherwise violates a rich heritage of doctrinal freedom.

After asserting that "one of the most disturbing developments in recent years has been a move toward creedalism in Southern Baptist life," Yarbrough claimed that he "could cite numerous examples of creeping creedalism and doctrinal legalism in Southern Baptist life," such as the SBC Peace Committee Report of 1987.[37]

CONCLUDING OBSERVATIONS

The SBC created a creedal trap for itself through a series of easy-to-discover steps.

First, a key event, perhaps unwittingly, set in motion creedal possibilities in Southern Baptist theological education. The Southern Baptist Theological Seminary included a confessional statement, the Abstract of Principles, in the fundamental Laws of the Seminary, written into its charter in 1858. That Abstract, required of professors teaching there since 1858, notes that every professor shall "teach in accordance with, and not contrary to, the Abstract of Principles." Then the Abstract itself includes the following sentence adapted from the *Second London* and *Philadelphia Confessions of Faith*: "God alone is Lord of the conscience, and He hath left it free from the doctrines and commandments of men, which are in anything contrary to His Word, or not contained in it."[38]

These contrasting emphases have created tensions for professors for decades. And the same tensions have developed in all SBC agencies that eventually adopted a confession of any kind and urged it upon employees. Logically, a person cannot have a conscience free from the doctrines of men and simultaneously teach according to a set of doctrines created by men with which he/she may not agree. That pattern feeds the possibility of creedalism and forces professors into inconsistencies between subscribed belief required for employment and actual faith.

Second, perhaps without deliberate intent, another development provided for the eventual possibility of creedalistic application in foreign missions. In 1920 the SBC Foreign Mission Board (FMB), predecessor of the IMB, adopted a doctrinal statement to guide its missionary appointees. The FMB built a powerful sense of expectation into the statement: "All missionaries of the Foreign Mission Board of the Southern Baptist Convention are expected to read carefully and subscribe to the following statement of belief [not reprinted here] before they are appointed to missionary service under the Board."[39]

Even though the possibility for a creedalistic application existed, it was not activated in that form in foreign missions until the twenty-first century and the advent of the *BFM2000*.

Third, the SBC adopted the *Baptist Faith and Message* in 1925 in response to such issues as evolution, modernism, and biblical inspiration.

The convention had held to an anti-confessional position for eighty years since its founding in 1845. Several factors had accounted for such opposition to confessions: (1) the influence of Separate Baptists, the Campbellite movement, and Landmarkism; (2) the nature and purpose of the SBC which opposed creating *The* Southern Baptist Church; and (3) the spirit of individualism cultivated on the American frontier and within southern culture.[40] Therefore, the adoption of a confession made creedalism possible by supplying a set of specific doctrines that theoretically could be used in negative ways.

Fourth, the SBC adopted a revised edition of the *Baptist Faith and Message* in 1963. The 1962 resolution calling for the writing of this statement included new language: that it "may serve as guidelines to the various agencies of the Southern Baptist Convention."[41] That offered brand new opportunities for forcing a confession on denominational employees, and agencies gradually fell into the trap of requiring employees to sign their agreement with this confession.

Fifth, in March, 1973, a group of Southern Baptists meeting in First Baptist Church, Atlanta, Georgia, voted to create the Baptist Faith and Message Fellowship (BFMF). They chartered the organization in Georgia in September of that year with M. O. Owens of North Carolina as president of a twenty-four-member board. The journal of the BFMF, *The Southern Baptist Journal*, edited by William A. Powell in 1973–1979, widely perpetuated the views of the BFMF. The BFMF "sought to convince all Southern Baptists to embrace its views of biblical orthodoxy" and "endeavored to expose Southern Baptist leaders who . . . advocated views unacceptable to the BFMF," such as its heavy emphasis on biblical inerrancy.[42] H. Leon McBeth claimed that "in function, this organization bore remarkable similarity to the old fundamentalist Fellowship in the Northern Baptist Convention."[43] The Fellowship basically institutionalized creedalism and promoted it as the norm for denominational strategies.

Sixth, several factors merged to lock the SBC into a creedalistic mind-set beginning in the late 1970s and continuing into the present: (1) the influence of the late Texas pastor W. A. Criswell as the theological godfather of the fundamentalist movement; (2) the success of Paul Pressler and Paige Patterson, both of Texas, in convincing messengers at SBC meetings to approve their techniques for controlling SBC doctrinal and political processes; (3) the 1979 election of Adrian Rogers as SBC president, followed by an unending succession of fundamentalist SBC presidents since that year; (4) the adoption of the SBC Peace Committee Report in 1987, which included the 1986 Glorieta Statement adopted by the six SBC seminary presidents; (5) the employment of Morris Chapman as president/CEO of the SBC Executive Committee in 1992; (6) the 1994 report of the SBC Presidential Theological Study Committee; (7) the reorganization of the SBC effective in 1997; (8) the 1998 revision of the *Baptist Faith and Message*; (9) the naming of fundamentalist trustees and CEOs for all SBC agencies; and (10) the systematic firing and early retiring of hundreds of denominational employees who refused to buy into the new theological and political system.

Seventh, the SBC adoption of the 2000 revision of the *Baptist Faith and Message,* whose preamble described confessions as "instruments of doctrinal accountability," successfully completed the SBC voyage into the harbor of creedalism. No professional denominational employee who refuses to abide by it is safe. Those who object can count on joining the ranks of hundreds who have already been theologically pink-slipped in the past twenty years.

This chapter will end in vain if it does not briefly address three basic questions: (1) Why has the SBC chosen to become a creedal convention when virtually all of its key documents on confessions vigorously oppose creedalism? (2) If inerrancy of the Bible as the sole written authority for Baptists has—according to SBC leaders—been the driving force of the "Conservative Resurgence" or SBC "Takeover," why have they now given priority to the *Baptist Faith and Message,* which is so non-inerrant that the SBC has changed it frequently in recent years? (3) What do these obvious inconsistencies at the heart of the denomination's identity say about SBC integrity?

The answers roll into a simple response.

Control has been the name of the SBC game; inerrancy has been nothing but a side issue. Pivotal documents and principles of Baptist history mean nothing to persons determined to capture the agencies and capital assets of a denomination without regard to who suffers. A critical weapon in this process has been to erect required, increasingly detailed, doctrinal parameters, then dismiss everyone who refuses to comply. Hypocrisy moves this process forward.

Creedalism is the bread and butter of fundamentalism, and fundamentalism is a contemporary Southern Baptist nightmare. It is a system of religion that fears freedom, demands control, and cracks down on nonconformity. "The ultimate characteristic that has distinguished fundamentalists from other evangelicals has been their insistence that there *can be* tests of faith. Fundamentalists insist on uniformity of belief within the ranks and separation from others whose beliefs and lives are suspect."[44]

Baptists of today may find it helpful to revisit their history. Baptists have used confessions for almost 400 years. But they have typically held firmly to three key points: (1) It is wrong to make a confession a substitute for the Bible. (2) It is equally wrong to force a confession on anyone. (3) It is right to use confessions consistently within the Baptist heritage of freedom.

The ultimate defining characteristic of Baptists who take seriously the life and teachings of Christ is a healthy respect for the freedom of individual faith. Baptist efforts to regulate their corporate life through covenants, community, and discipline, apart from intense appreciation for the right of personal choice, run counter to Jesus' careful cultivation of personal dignity. There is no room in the Kingdom of God to force corporate doctrinal judgments on individuals. There is no place in Baptist life to override personal decision-making in deference to creedal authority. Baptists ought to squash every attempt to bind the saints with pliers of compliance.

A powerful argument against creedalism is that theological variety has characterized Baptist confessional statements since the early 1600s. Whose confession is right? Confessions differ because Baptists differ—chronologically, geographically, racially, ethnically, culturally, socioeconomically. Every confession reflects the crises of the time; the personalities, training, and prejudices of the writers; accurate or inaccurate understandings of the role of confessions and creedalism in Baptist history; and assorted other factors.

Every Baptist confession will someday date itself; therefore, no justification exists for creedalizing it. The earliest Baptists were right; confessions can have positive uses. The Separate Baptists were also right; every confession should be approached cautiously; someone might try to turn it against you.

NOTES

[1] Morris H. Chapman, "New Vision, Voices, Victories!" *SBC Life* (April 2002) 1.

[2] W. Morgan Patterson, "The Baptist Heritage: An Occasion for Gratitude," *The Fibers of Our Faith: The Herschel H. and Frances J. Hobbs Lectureship in Baptist Faith and Heritage at Oklahoma Baptist University*, ed. Dick Allen Rader (Franklin TN: Providence House Publishers, 1995) 32.

[3] H. Leon McBeth, *The Baptist Heritage: Four Centuries of Baptist Witness* (Nashville: Broadman Press, 1987) 686.

[4] William L. Lumpkin, *Baptist Confessions of Faith*, rev. ed. (Valley Forge: Judson Press, 1969) 115, 119.

[5] Ibid., 158.

[6] Ibid., 191.

[7] Ibid., 248, 279-80.

[8] Ibid., 362.

[9] *Annual*, Southern Baptist Convention, 1925, 71.

[10] *Annual*, Southern Baptist Convention, 1963, 269-70.

[11] "Report of the Baptist Faith and Message Study Committee to the Southern Baptist Convention, Adopted June 14th, 2000," in <www.SBC.net> (2 April 2002) 1, 2, 3.

[12] Lumpkin, *Baptist Confessions of Faith*, 382.

[13] Howard Wayne Smith, "Baptists and Creeds," *The Chronicle* VII (April 1944): 58.

[14] W. J. McGlothlin, *Baptist Confessions of Faith* (Boston: American Baptist Publication Society, 1911) 57.

[15] Ibid., 334, 343.

[16] G. Keith Parker, *Baptists in Europe: History & Confessions of Faith* (Nashville: Broadman Press, 1982) 57.

[17] Edward Bean Underhill, ed., *Confessions of Faith, and Other Public Documents, Illustrative of the History of the Baptist Churches of England in the 17th Century* (Edited for The Hanserd Knollys Society; London: Haddon, Brothers and Co., 1854) vi.

[18] McGlothlin, *Baptist Confessions of Faith*, xi.

[19] Ibid., xii.

[20] Lumpkin, *Baptist Confessions of Faith*, 17.

[21] William L. Lumpkin, "Confessions of Faith, Baptist," *Encyclopedia of Southern Baptists*, I (Nashville: Broadman Press, 1958) 305-306.

[22] Parker, *Baptists in Europe*, 20.

[23] Ibid., 11-12.

[24] Ibid., 12.

[25] James E. Carter, "American Baptist Confessions of Faith: A Review of Confessions of Faith Adopted by Major Baptist Bodies in the United States," *The Lord's Free People in a Free Land: Essays in Baptist History in Honor of Robert A. Baker*, ed. William R. Estep (Fort Worth: Faculty, School of Theology, Southwestern Baptist Theological Seminary, 1976) 55.

[26] James E. Carter, "Baptists Affirm Their Faith" (Nashville: Historical Commission, SBC, 1979) panel 2.

[27] E. Glenn Hinson, "Confessions or Creeds in Early Christian Tradition," *Review and Expositor* LXXVI (Winter 1979): 15.

[28] Bill J. Leonard, "Types of Confessional Documents Among Baptists," *Review and Expositor* LXXVI (Winter 1979): 41.

[29] William H. Brackney, *Historical Dictionary of the Baptists*, Historical Dictionaries of Religions, Philosophies, and Movements, No. 25 (Lanham MD: Scarecrow Press, 1999) 111.

[30] Bob R. Agee, "Southern Baptists and the Tensions That Shape Us," *The Fibers of Our Faith*, 63.

[31] Herschel H. Hobbs, "The People Called Baptists: Whence, Who, What, Whither," *The Fibers of Our Faith*, 17, 19-21, 24-25.

[32] Herschel H. Hobbs, "The Baptist Faith and Message," *The Fibers of Our Faith*, 70, 73.

[33] Herschel H. Hobbs, "Southern Baptist Convention: The Inerrancy Controversy," *The Fibers of Our Faith*, 121.

[34] See *Annual*, Southern Baptist Convention, 1845, 19.

[35] Walter B. Shurden, "Theological Erosion of Southern Baptist Distinctives," *The Fibers of Our Faith*, 141-43.

[36] Robert A. Baker, "Divided We Stand," *The Fibers of Our Faith*, 149-54.

[37] Slayden A. Yarbrough, "Baptists and Freedom: Conviction and Contradiction," *The Fibers of Our Faith*, 162-63, 168.

[38] William A. Mueller, *A History of Southern Baptist Theological Seminary* (Nashville: Broadman Press, 1959) 238, 240.

[39] *Annual*, Southern Baptist Convention, 1920, 196.

[40] Walter B. Shurden, "Southern Baptist Responses to Their Confessional Statements," *Review and Expositor* LXXVI (Winter 1979): 69-71.

[41] *Annual*, Southern Baptist Convention, 1962, 64.

[42] Bob D. Compton, "Baptist Faith and Message Fellowship, The," *Encyclopedia of Southern Baptists*, IV (Nashville: Broadman Press, 1982) 2, 101.

[43] H. Leon McBeth, *A Sourcebook for Baptist Heritage* (Nashville: Broadman Press, 1990) 519.

[44] Nancy T. Ammerman, "North American Protestant Fundamentalism," in *Fundamentalisms Observed*, ed. Martin E. Marty and R. Scott Appleby (Chicago: University of Chicago Press, 1991) 7-8.

TEXAS BAPTISTS TAKE A STAND

BY CHARLES WADE

[Ed Note: This chapter is adapted from remarks made by Charles Wade, executive director of the Baptist General Convention of Texas, to the Executive Board of the BGCT on February 26, 2002. The Executive Board followed up that day with two historic actions: (1) establishing a Chaplaincy Endorsement Board open to all qualified men and women and (2) launching a fund to cover transition expenses of any Southern Baptist missionary who resigned or might be fired for refusal to sign an affirmation of the 2000 Baptist Faith and Message. Eighteen prominent Texas Baptists gave the fund a running start with combined pledges of $1 million..]

Within one week, the week before the Texas Baptist Evangelism Conference, I was in three churches—two celebrating ten years as two of our 2000 new church starts, and another just moving into a new building. One was an African American congregation in Missouri City, Texas; another a multi-racial middle-class church in the United community of north Laredo; another in east Arlington, where social difficulties abound. Each church will mediate grace and mercy, salvation and hope to broken and lost lives.

What Texas Baptists are about every day, 365 days a year, is reaching out to people, praying for and seeking the lost, starting new churches, creating ministries of compassion, caring for families, and strengthening our twenty-three institutions that prepare our young people for service and leadership, that minister to children who have been thrown away, that care for the aged, and that minister physical and spiritual healing to the sick. We also focus on assisting our churches to be vital, healthy, grace-giving communities of faith; working with associations as they equip their churches to fulfill the Great Commission; and, to sum up, assisting the churches and related ministries to be the presence of Christ in the world.

During this time, preparing for the Evangelism Conference and visiting in our churches, came the word. . . . A letter from the chief executive officer of the Southern Baptist Convention's Executive Committee [Morris Chapman] has been received in our churches asking them to change their giving to favor the Southern Baptist Convention (SBC) against the Baptist General Convention of Texas (BGCT).

Then, within just a few days, a letter came from some missionary friends telling me of a letter from the International Mission Board (IMB) president [Jerry Rankin] urging them to sign the 2000 *Baptist Faith and Message* (*BFM2000*) in order to protect them from charges of heresy and to strengthen the mission board. They were hurt and afraid: "What can you do to help us and others who will not be able to sign this document?"

To be candid, I was dismayed and frustrated. Why now? Why do they continue to push us to defend ourselves and to speak up for what is right and fair in Baptist life? Why would the president of the IMB do something he had promised us he would not do? Pastors began to call and e-mail: "How can this be?" "I thought it would never come to this." "My church needs a way to help the missionaries." "What can we do about this?"

The letter from the SBC Executive Committee asked Texas Baptist churches to choose a 50/50 split in Cooperative Program giving. This was unprecedented. I express appreciation to the Texas Woman's Missionary Union for publicly asking the Executive Committee of the SBC to refrain from seeking to directly influence our Texas Baptist churches in their decisions regarding the giving of funds.

Interestingly, when the Cooperative Program was established in 1927, the goal was for the states to raise approximately one dollar for Southern Baptist causes for each dollar they raised for their state mission program. That is, they were hopeful for a 50/50 division of mission dollars. But the [Cooperative Program] document specifically called for the dollars raised in the two SBC mission offerings—the Lottie Moon Offering for Foreign Missions and the Annie Armstrong Offering for Home Missions—to be counted in that 50/50 ratio.

The truth is that for many years the BGCT has, when the two large mission offerings are counted, contributed 50 percent of our offering receipts to Southern Baptist causes. Not one word about that was mentioned in the letter from the Executive Committee. Just this past year, in spite of the distractions and in spite of a rebel convention [the Southern Baptists of Texas Convention (SBTC)] siphoning off support from Texas ministries, the BGCT contributed 46 percent of our total offering receipts to Southern Baptist causes. We have been generous in our support. We have supported more institutions than any other state, out of the generosity of our Texas Baptist people and their churches. Such an attack on the integrity of our Texas Baptist adopted budget was improper, mean-spirited, and ungrateful. To add to the wrong, a four-color promotional piece was included in the letter, touting the competing convention [SBTC] in Texas. And all of this was paid for out of Cooperative Program funds, which our own Texas Baptist churches have helped to give. *[Ed. note: The SBTC was formed to align with the SBC but not the BGCT.]*

Now, permit me to say a word about the letter from the president of the IMB to the missionaries. In this letter the missionaries are urged to affirm the *BFM2000*.

There are many who feel strongly that those being supported by the denomination should be willing to pledge affirmation and support for the current BF&M, especially those serving with the mission boards. Failure to ask for this affirmation is creating suspicion that there are IMB personnel whose beliefs and practices are inconsistent with those represented by Southern Baptists.

. . . there have not been major changes to the document. . . . Signing this affirmation protects you from charges of heresy behind your back while you are overseas and cannot defend yourself. (Italics mine)

The next week, in an attempt to soften the tone of the first letter, the president of the IMB, speaking to state Baptist editors, said it was "pure speculation" that missionaries would have to resign if they would not sign the *BFM2000*; they would not be fired for noting their exceptions to the document. However, he said that the IMB leaders have not determined what the consequences would be for missionaries who cannot sign the statement of affirmation. "We may have to deal with that in the future."

He continued by saying that he hopes no "minor detail of disagreement" would prevent someone called by God from fulfilling his or her missionary assignment. "To me, it is untenable that a person would be disobedient to their call. . . ."

We have no reason to feel comfortable that the missionaries are not now under serious attack from their own administrators and board. We have reason to believe that the IMB trustees will press to remove these missionaries if the president does not do so. After all, we have the example of what happened to one of the regional leaders who had to resign because he would not sign. But it is not just what we read when we read the letters and remarks. It is what the missionaries believe is being said to them. You will hear later [during the Executive Board meeting] some of the appeals of the missionaries in their own words. Words that compelled us to call our Missions Review and Initiatives Committee together to study this matter and prepare a report to the Executive Board of the BGCT. [This report came later in the meeting.]

We would be happy if the IMB should respond to our call for them to pull back from this forcing upon faithful, long-term missionaries a confession of faith, which is being used as a creed. But we must put in place a response mechanism now. We will not meet again until late May [2002]. We need to begin to build a fund to help these missionaries, who are saying to us they will have to resign or take early retirement under this pressure. *[Ed. note: Later in the meeting, the BGCT Executive Board approved the launching of a fund to help resigning missionaries with transition expenses.]*

There are many questions and not enough answers today. But the call to stand by those who are being asked to put either their calling or their conscience at risk cannot go unanswered. We must provide places of refuge and renewal, places of warm acceptance and dependable support, places where dreams of serving God can become reality again. I believe Texas Baptist churches and people want to do this, and they want us to help them find a way to do it.

Bill Pinson [former BGCT executive director] wrote me last week and observed, "Opportunities often come to us disguised as challenges or problems." I believe that is exactly where Texas Baptists stand now. I have asked myself, "Charles, if you do not stand beside these missionaries, if you do not speak up when they are being pressed down by this fundamentalist mind-set that places heavy burdens down upon men and women's shoulders, then you have no right to open your mouth again about how Baptists believe in the priesthood of the believer, soul competency, religious liberty, and the freedom of the Christian soul."

Where in the Scripture is it ever recorded that men and women were required to sign a confession of faith or a creed? We are called to give testimony. We are required to give a reason for the faith that is within us. But there is nothing about signing some statement that a committee or a religious council has designed and insists you sign. Here is the Scripture: 1 Peter 3:15-16a. "But in your hearts set apart Christ as Lord. Always be prepared to give an answer to everyone who asks you to give the reason for the hope that you have. But do this with gentleness and respect, keeping a clear conscience. . . ."

There are three other serious matters, which I will only address briefly.

First, the BGCT has instituted a program of staff deployment in which we will be very active in being present in the field, working with our churches and associations. We want the people and churches of Texas to know our hearts and to feel free to ask help of us in meeting the challenges of their communities and cities. We are calling this, "Building Relationships: 2002." I have said to our staff, "I want somebody who works for the BGCT Executive Board to know somebody in every church." We want to strengthen directors of missions, pastors and church staff, and the laity of our congregations by being there with and for you. We want to link up with you, not only the resources of the Baptist Building but also the resources of our Baptist institutions across Texas.

Second, a resolution regarding the Scriptures will come from the BGCT Administrative Committee. *[Ed. note: That resolution was approved later in the meeting.]* You have, in that report in your materials, a wonderful statement about our Texas Baptist commitment to the Word of God. Let no one doubt the joyful gratitude we express to God for his written Word. It is a lamp to our feet and a light for our path (Psalm 19:105). "The grass withers and the flowers fall, but the word of our God stands forever" (Isaiah 40:8). It "is the record of God's revelation of Himself to man. It is a perfect treasure of divine instruction" (*BFM1963*).

Let no one doubt our adoration for and praise to the Son of God, our Savior, who is the Living Word of God (John 1:1, 14). When we open the inspired word of God and handle with our trembling hands the Holy Bible that it might speak God's truth and the way of salvation to our hearts and minds, we listen to the Holy Spirit as he guides us into all truth, and we rejoice that the Holy Spirit teaches us through Jesus the Christ, who becomes the hermeneutical standard, the norm for our faith, the criterion by which we know how God wants us to understand and interpret the Bible.

We have tried to be kind in our defense of the *BFM1963* statement regarding the Bible, in comparison with the *BFM2000*. But dear people, it is simply wrong not to acknowledge what the Bible clearly shows—Jesus is the revelation of God to man, not the Bible. The Bible is "*the*"—not "a," not "just any"—but "*the*" inspired and written record of God's revelation of Himself to man. But it is about Jesus that the Scriptures say: ". . . in these last days he has spoken to us by his Son, whom he appointed heir of all things, and through whom he made the universe. The Son is the radiance of God's glory and the exact representation of his being, sustaining all things by his powerful word. After he had pro-vided purification for sins, he sat down at the right hand of the Majesty in heaven" (Hebrews 1:2-3).

We celebrate with reverence the gift of God to us in the inspired Scriptures. We believe the Book that is in our hands. We believe it so much that we need no man-made summaries to take its place. If you want a creed, it is perfectly right for you to write one. Review it with trusted Christian teachers. Refine it. Test it by Scripture. Live with it. Teach it. But don't put it down before another Christian brother or sister and insist that they say their faith exactly the way you say yours. Learn from one another. Challenge one another. Most of all, really listen to one another. And in prayer God will teach us in Scripture more than we knew and enough to help one another know Christ and grow up into his likeness.

Third, the BGCT Administrative Committee will bring a recommendation that we approve the establishment of a Chaplaincy Endorsement Board. *[Ed. note: The recommen-dation was approved later in the meeting.]* This has been in the works for some time because chaplains were being told that the North American Mission Board would not continue to renew their endorsement if they would not sign off on the *BFM2000*. For all the reasons mentioned above, they asked us for help.

Just this past week [early February, 2002], yet another restriction was handed down. Any women who have been ordained to the ministry will no longer be acceptable for endorsement as chaplains by the North American Mission Board. This means that women chaplains who serve in hospitals, the military, women's prisons, etc., can no longer serve as Baptist chaplains unless they can secure an endorsement from some other Baptist body. We were ready to move forward [with the Chaplaincy Endorsement Board] before we knew this particular decision would be made.

I am aware that we will be criticized by many for the stands we are being asked to take today. Some will say that we are distancing ourselves from Southern Baptists. Let me say again, as I have said before, we stand ready to work with Southern Baptists. We have not wanted the things that have happened in the last few weeks to happen. We are focused on a lost world that needs our Savior and his gospel. Why these distractions? Why these extra requirements?

If we or the missionaries are heretics, show us by Scripture and we will repent. But if you cannot say we are heretics, then work with us for the sake of a world that needs Jesus. And let us all thank God for however we heard the gospel and were saved, though it came from a man or a woman, from a Jew or a Gentile, from bond or free. For when we miss Hell and enter into glory we will want to find those who helped us know Jesus and thank them every one, and we will wonder then that we thought we could tell people what the Sovereign God could or could not do with their lives.

WHICH WORD DO WE WORSHIP?

BY BRUCE PRESCOTT

Southern Baptist Convention (SBC) leaders have reduced biblical interpretation to a corpus of mummified dogmas. At the heart of their dogmatism lies the same desire for security that underlies all forms of idolatry. Many Baptists will resent those incendiary words, but the evidence speaks for itself. That sad state of affairs results when Christians forget to put first things first.

As a child at Vacation Bible School, I pledged allegiance to the American flag, the Christian flag, and the Bible—in that order. From an early age I was taught to cherish each of those, and I still love and respect what each of them represents. As I grew older, however, I learned to make distinctions and weigh values and the ordering of my allegiances shifted.

Today, my allegiance to Christ always comes first.

When I was a teenager growing up in an independent, fundamentalist Baptist church, we often sang a chorus I first learned as a child in VBS: "The B-I-B-L-E, Yes, that's the book for me, I'll stand alone on the word of God, the B-I-B-L-E." More often than that, I heard preachers pound on the pulpit and lift their Bibles high and forcefully thunder out rhetoric such as: "All we know about Jesus is in this book. If the Bible is not infallible and inerrant, then nobody, nobody, nobody can tell us how to get to God for sure."[1]

At that time, it seemed clear to me that if you did not believe the Bible, you could not be saved. The Bible's inerrancy served to "guarantee" that the Christian faith was true. Without it you could not be sure of your salvation. In essence, you had to pledge allegiance to the Bible before you could pledge allegiance to Christ. As I grew older and my faith and my thinking matured, however, the ordering of my allegiances shifted.

Today, my allegiance to Christ always comes first.

THE PRIORITY OF CHRIST

I learned to put Christ first in all things the hard way. When I witnessed to my friends, our discussions would almost inevitably bog down on matters that I now know are unnecessary for salvation. Conversations rarely reached the point at which the love that God demonstrated to us through Jesus could be discussed. Instead, endless debates about the historical and scientific veracity of the Scriptures were common. It grieves me that people turned away from faith in Christ because I left them with the impression that salvation involved believing in a young earth and creation science. I believe it grieves God, too.

After reflecting on experiences in which I actually led people to the Lord, I began to perceive the error in what many well-meaning but misguided preachers told me. I never found any unbeliever who responded favorably to arguments about the infallibility and inerrancy of the Bible. People did favorably receive a testimony about Jesus and about the difference that having a personal relationship with him makes in life. I also discovered that when you put first things first, other things fall into place. Those who put their faith in Jesus did not need to be convinced about the authority of the Bible; they seemed genuinely eager to study the Bible and learn more about their Savior.

These experiences made me cautious about the tendency in many Baptist churches to overemphasize the Bible at the expense of Jesus. Now, Baptists leaders have escalated that tendency to epidemic levels with the changes to the article on the Scriptures in the 2000 *Baptist Faith and Message (BFM2000)*.

THE SUPREME REVELATION OF GOD

BFM1925 simply described the Bible as "a perfect treasure of heavenly instruction." There was no discussion of "God's revelation" in that version of the BFM.

BFM1963 added a sentence discussing "God's revelation." In that version the Bible is described as "the record of God's revelation of himself to man." The words "the record of" made it clear that Christ always comes first and that the Bible, as indispensable as it certainly is, should not be regarded as the supreme revelation of God. God's supreme revelation is by incarnation—in the person of Jesus Christ. The Bible is "the record of" the good news that God loved us enough to reveal himself personally.

BFM2000, in effect, demotes Jesus and promotes the Bible. The framers removed the words "the record of" from the sentence about revelation in the article on Scriptures. Here the Bible alone is identified as God's revelation.[2] What is being obscured is the good news that God loved us enough to reveal himself to us personally in Jesus Christ.

The revisers of the *BFM2000* allege that defining the Bible as "the record of" God's revelation is code word for "neo-orthodox" theology. In reality, it expresses the biblical theology of the epistle to the Hebrews:

> In the past God spoke to our forefathers through the prophets at many times and in various ways, but in these last days he has spoken to us by his Son, . . . The Son is the radiance of God's glory and the exact representation of his being. (Heb 1:1-3)

Hebrews clearly accentuates the priority that must be given to God's revelation by incarnation. Spoken words and sacred writings may give a glimpse of God's glory and a hint of his being, but they can never radiate his glory or exactly represent his being. God is not an idea or concept. No words are adequate to describe him. Our only hope to know him truly is for God to reveal himself to us personally.[3] That is why *the Word* that *was with God and . . . was God . . . became flesh, and dwelt among us* (John 1:1, 14).

This is important. Our belief in the incarnation of God in Jesus distinguishes our faith from other faiths. Belief in the authority of sacred writings is not unique to the Christian faith. Other monotheistic religions affirm the words spoken *to our forefathers through the prophets*, and some modern cults affirm that God *has spoken to us by his Son*, as well as through the writings of certain latter-day "prophets." It is pointless to compete with such religions on the basis of each faith's relative ability to secure fidelity to a scriptural authority.

For Christians, revelation is ultimately personal (incarnate Word), not propositional (written words). What is unique to the Christian faith is our belief that God revealed himself fully, finally, and completely in Jesus Christ. Only Christians believe that *in these last days* God reveals himself through a Son, the living "Word of God," who radiates the glory of his sacrificial love and exactly represents his holy presence.

Contrary to what the *BFM2000* revisers claim, giving priority to revelation by incarnation does not diminish the importance of the words spoken to the prophets or written by the apostles. It simply acknowledges what Scriptures themselves proclaim—that the authority and effect of their words is derivative; living only as the Spirit unveils their meaning and inscribes it on human hearts.[4]

In contrast, the authority and effect of the living "Word of God" is absolute:

> The Word of God is living and active and sharper than any two edged sword, and piercing as far as the division of soul and spirit, of both joints and marrow, and able to judge the thoughts and intentions of the heart *and there is no creature hidden from His sight, but all things are open and laid bare to the eyes of Him with whom we have to do.* (Heb 4:12-13; italics mine)

The passage above has been quoted out of context so many times that most people think it refers to the written Scriptures rather than to Jesus—the "living Word." This error probably explains why so many Baptists are willing to elevate the Bible at the expense of Jesus.

"WORD OF GOD": ALIVE, NOT DEAD

People have long described the Bible "metaphorically" as the "Word of God," both out of reverence for the scriptural records of God's self-revelation and as an acknowledgement of the privileged place the Bible holds in showing us the way God encounters us. This way of describing the Scriptures, however, has obscured the biblical usage of the phrase "Word of God" and made it a "dead metaphor."

"Dead metaphors" are phrases that are understood automatically—without thinking—by simple mental associations. Too many Christians automatically associate "Word of God" with the Bible rather than thinking that it points to Jesus.

The Bible almost always employs living metaphors that cannot be understood by automatic mental associations. Understanding living metaphors requires thought. There is a tension in living metaphors that points to a meaning that is greater than can be conveyed by simple, unthinking mental associations.[5] With few exceptions, the phrase "Word of God," as used in Scripture, means much more than simply "Bible" or "written word."

In Scripture, the "Word of God" is *living and active* (Heb 4:12-13) or *living and abiding* (1 Pet 1:23). Jesus likened the "Word of God" to a *seed* that is planted and grows in a heart (Luke 8:11). After Pentecost, Luke wrote that the Word of God *increased* (Acts 6:7) and *grew and multiplied* (Acts 12:24). Most of the Bible verses about the Word of God relate to the dynamic spiritual processes involved in "preaching," "hearing," or "receiving" the "good news" about Jesus. John's Revelation talks about one who is *clothed with a robe dipped in blood; and His name is called The Word of God* (Rev 19:13).

In almost every biblical instance, "Word of God" is best understood as a "living metaphor" that points beyond the "written word" to the "living Word." Most significant is the fact that, in the one instance in which Jesus used the metaphor "word of God" in a sense that primarily referenced Scripture, he was complaining that the *traditions* of men had rendered the word *of none effect* (Mark 7:13).

No stronger denunciation of creedalism has ever been given. The traditions of men negated what God told Isaiah when he said that the word *shall not return unto me empty, without accomplishing that which I desire, and without succeeding in the matter for which I sent it* (Isa 55:11).

Apparently, one thing can empty God's Word and make it *of none effect*. The framers of *BFM2000* did that openly when they removed the "wiggle room"[6] for thought that is created by "living metaphors" and replaced them with the "dead metaphors" of creedal interpretations.

This causes automatic mental associations to fill the place where the "living Word" speaks to the heart and soul and mind. The "tradition" codified in *BFM2000* usurps the place of the "Word of God." Nothing makes that more apparent than the other significant change to the article on Scriptures in *BFM2000*—removing Christ as the criterion for interpreting the Scriptures.

THE CRITERION FOR INTERPRETATION

BFM1963 added a sentence that highlighted the Lordship of Christ over the process of interpreting the Bible. It said, "The criterion by which the Bible is to be interpreted is Jesus Christ." This is a principle of interpretive humility that reminds us of our individual and collective fallibility. No mortal and no "blue ribbon committee"—no matter how learned or devout—can presume anything approaching infallibility or finality for their interpretations of the Bible. Christ alone interprets Scripture infallibly. Every interpreter and every interpretation falls short when measured by the authority of Jesus.

That is why Baptists have historically refused to affirm creeds or permit confessions of faith to become "instruments of doctrinal accountability," as now stated in *BFM2000's* preamble. Confessions of faith are not "the criterion by which the Bible is to be interpreted." Jesus Christ is the criterion by which the Bible is to be interpreted. *BFM2000* deleted the "criterion" sentence and replaced it with the statement that "All Scripture is a testimony to Christ, who is Himself the focus of divine revelation."

This makes it perfectly clear that Jesus is no longer being regarded as God's revelation; he has been demoted to merely "the focus of divine revelation." It is equally clear that the process by which the "living Word" (through the presence of the Holy Spirit) guides every believer to interpret the Bible has been made *of none effect*. The "wiggle room," where the resurrected "living Word" had space to "breathe"[7] life into the Scriptures, has been removed.

So, convinced that they are preserving the "Word of God," Southern Baptists are shrouding the Bible within the lifeless corpus of their own "traditions" and burying it in the vacuum-sealed tomb of *BFM2000*.

This is not the first time that dead letters have been preferred to the promptings of the life-giving Spirit. Some people naturally prefer letters written with *ink* or on *tablets of stone* to letters written by the *Spirit* on *tablets of human hearts* (2 Cor 3:2-18). Not convinced that the "living Word" is adequate to *judge the thoughts and intentions of the heart* (Heb 4:12-13), these people insist that *BFM2000's* interpretation of "Scripture stands in judgment of my experience, not my experience in judgment of Scripture."[8]

That is why, for many Southern Baptists, *a veil lies over their heart* whenever they read about the works of the Holy Spirit in the Scriptures. They are deaf to the passages that say *your daughters shall prophesy* (Joel 2:28-29; Acts 2:17). They are blind to examples of the early church giving greater weight to evidences of spiritual experience than to *the custom taught by Moses* (Acts 8:26-38; 10:1-48; 15:1-29). They would ignore Peter's precedent-setting conclusion that *God, who knows the heart, bore witness to them, giving them the Holy Spirit, just as He also did to us* (Acts 15:8).

Lacking the spiritual discernment necessary to read the Bible and walk by faith under the Lordship of Christ, many Southern Baptists have indeed reduced biblical interpretation to a corpus of mummified dogmas. This dogmatism springs from the same desire for security that underlies every form of idolatry.

MAKING THE BIBLE AN IDOL

All idols respond to the human desire for a substantial basis for faith. Every idol represents an attempt to limit God, control him, and put him at man's disposal. Early idols were crude attempts to "handle" and control God by means of graven images made of wood or stone or precious metal. God prohibited the making of all such images and idols because he is sovereign and free. He resists every effort to limit him, define him, or reduce his place in our lives. God refuses to be controlled, manipulated, or put at our disposal.

As people set aside crude attempts at controlling God, idolatry took on more subtle and sophisticated forms. Scripture records the progressive development of idolatry toward its more sophisticated forms.

The Ark of the Covenant became an idol when, after a skirmish with the Philistines, the sons of Eli brought the Ark to the battlefield to assure that the Lord would *come among us and deliver us from the power of our enemies* (1 Sam 4:3). But God would not be manipulated; he let the Philistines capture the Ark.

The Temple became an idol when, in the days of Jeremiah, Judah refused to repent and trusted false prophets, who said, *This is the Temple of the Lord* (Jer 7:1-14). They were certain that God would never let Jerusalem fall to the Babylonians. But God has never been confined to *dwell in houses made by human hands* (Acts 7:48). He let the Babylonians capture Jerusalem and tear down the Temple.

The Law became an idol when, in the time of Christ, the Pharisees and Sadducees were so secure in its truth and so certain of its meaning that they used it to condemn Jesus.[9] God cannot be limited and defined by written words and legal precepts.[10] He took the curse of the law upon himself, and broke it, so that we might know his grace and live by faith in freedom.[11]

The developing sophistication of idolatry did not end in biblical times. Throughout the history of the church it has continued, in varying forms, to the present day. Its most recent modern form is the elevation of the Bible over Jesus.

Like the Ark of the Covenant, the Temple, and the Law, the role of the Bible in the drama of divine redemption is vital. But reverence for the Bible and its authority must never divert attention from the central and preeminent place Christ holds in the drama of redemption and revelation. *There is one God, and one mediator between God and men, the man Christ Jesus* (1 Tim 2:5). Jesus alone is the ground and foundation for our faith.

A DIFFERENT GOSPEL

The Bible correctly warns us against the danger of preaching "another gospel" (Gal 1:6-9). Many Southern Baptists are perilously close to that.

Those who wrote and those who affirm *BFM2000* strenuously deny that they are making the Bible an idol. I doubt that any of them intend to do so. But neither do I believe that first-century Judaism ever intended to turn the Hebrew Bible into an idol. Innocent intentions, however, are no excuse for bad actions. Legalists among first-century Jews founded their faith so firmly on God's "written word" that they crucified God's "living Word." When those legalists stand before God, they will have no excuse. Neither will Southern Baptist legalists be excused for changing the proclamation of the "living Word of God" into rhetorical defenses of the "written word of God."

The preamble to *BFM2000* makes the changed gospel that Baptists are preaching explicit. The preamble to *BFM1963* proclaims that our "living faith" is "rooted and grounded in Jesus Christ." *BFM2000* deletes that language and replaces it with a testimony that "Our living faith is established upon eternal truths" and a witness to the veracity of the Bible: "In an age increasingly hostile to Christian truth, our challenge is to express the truth as revealed in Scripture."

The difference between these two gospels is rooted in divergent understandings of the nature and meaning of truth. *BFM1963* reflects the belief that truth is personal. *BFM2000* reflects the belief that truth is rational.

Truth is ultimately personal. Scriptures only record a fraction of the truth that God revealed in Jesus. Scripture itself says that if everything were written down, *even the whole world would not have room for the books that would be written* (John 21:25).

In the final analysis, truth cannot be identified with the cold, lifeless abstractions of reason and logic—even if that logic begins with precepts from the Bible. "Living faith" is not mental assent to "eternal truths." Living faith "is rooted and grounded in Jesus Christ" because *Jesus is the way, the truth and the life* (John 14:6).

Christians abide in a personal relationship of love and trust with the "Eternal Truth," not with a system of "eternal truths." Jesus embodies "Eternal Truth" and real faith can only be founded on a personal relationship with him. For us, "living faith" is a process of spiritual growth and maturation. The real depths of spiritual truth can be learned only by personally experiencing the guiding presence of *the Spirit of truth* (John 16:12-13). That is why the preamble to *BFM1963* emphasized that we "must experience a growing understanding of truth."

The revisers of *BFM2000* seem to be uncomfortable with processes of spiritual growth and discovery. Truth that is learned by experience—even by experience with God—is too subjective for them. For them, truth must be objective and rational. That is why they insist that "faith is established on eternal truths." Some people are never satisfied unless truth is frozen and reduced to timeless precepts and rational propositions. A faith founded on the Bible, rather than on the "living Word," requires that all God's "truth" be reduced to shapes that conform to what human minds can "handle" or "grasp."

THE TRUE FOUNDATION

This "new gospel," requiring faith in the Bible before sharing the "good news" about Jesus, springs from the desire to have a logically substantiated foundation for faith. The revisers of *BFM2000* want rational, objectively certain reasons for their faith. They believe that a perfect or inerrant Bible can secure the logical, objectively certain foundation they think will give them: (1) assurance of salvation, (2) irrefutable arguments for the existence of God, and (3) logically unassailable systems of theological thought. They surmise that this will give them the power to convert unbelievers by force of logic. History, however, shows that logic inevitably fails to produce many conversions. When logic fails, the logicians turn their attention to finding and justifying other ways of exercising force over the unconverted.

The logic of idolatry has always been one of power, not love.

The truth is, God will not be confined to a book he inspired to be written by human hands any more than he would be confined to a temple he led followers to construct with human hands. God cannot be limited and defined by the syllogisms of human logic and reasoning: *"My thoughts are not your thoughts, nor are your ways my ways," declares the Lord. "For as the heavens are higher than the earth, So are My ways higher than your ways and My thoughts than your thoughts"* (Isa 55:8-9). God's logic is beyond human logic. He always remains free and sovereign. His logic is one of superabundance. It always gives more and asks more than is reasonable or prudent.[12] God's logic is one of love and grace, not power.

The root of the entire problem stems from resting faith on the wrong foundation:

• The Christian faith has always been founded on Jesus, not the Bible.
• Long before the gospels were written, men and women believed in Jesus of Nazareth.
• A century and a half before the text of the Bible was compiled, people trusted Christ as their savior.
• A millennium and a half before Bibles were printed and widely distributed, men and women believed that Jesus was the Christ.

Almost all of these people were saved the old-fashioned way—by the witness and testimony of ordinary men and women who freely and faithfully shared their personal experiences with the living Christ.

Christ is the only sure foundation for faith, *For no one can lay any foundation other than the one already laid, which is Jesus Christ* (1 Cor 3:11). He alone can satisfy our inner hunger for certainty and security in life, and he does it on his own terms. He sent the Holy Spirit, not logic, to confirm the authority of the Bible and to guide us to all truth.[13]

In this life, we have no logical or objectively certain security. We only have an inner, subjective *assurance of things hoped for and the conviction of things not seen* that spring from the presence of the Spirit of Christ within our hearts (Heb 11:1).

To ask for more is to ask God to change the way he relates to humanity. People have always had to live by faith, rather than by sight, to be rightly related to God.

NOTES

[1] Cf. the statement that Baptist Press, the SBC public relations arm, reported that Southeastern Seminary President Paige Patterson made to students at Southeastern Seminary on August 26, 1999: "Friend, it is as logical as it can be, if we do not have a more sure word of prophecy from the Word of God, if we do not have the Word of the Lord, infallible and inerrant and absolutely trustworthy, then nobody, nobody, nobody who's ever lived, nobody who lives now, nobody who will ever live, has an answer that will tell us how to get to God for sure.'" This story was removed from the online archives for Baptist Press after my article, "SBC President Assigns Attributes of Deity to the Bible," appeared in the April 2000 issue of the *Mainstream Messenger*, <e.htm>.

[2] Consonant with this is a proclamation that former SBC president James Merritt is reported to have made in his sermon at the 2001 annual meeting of the SBC. David Flick, former director of missions for Grady Baptist Association in Oklahoma, quotes Merritt as saying about the Bible, "This book ALONE is the word of God!"

[3] John 14:6.

[4] 2 Corinthians 3:2-18.

[5] Cf. Paul Ricoeur, *The Rule of Metaphor* (Toronto: University of Toronto Press, 1977).

[6] In an address at Midwestern Seminary, then SBC President Paige Patterson referred to changes in the *BFM2000*, saying, "I'm glad we took it out. We needed to take away the wiggle room." See Baptist Press news story on 5 September 2000.

[7] Scriptures were written by *inspiration of God*; they are literally *theopneustos*— "God-breathed" (2 Tim 3:16). Interpreting Scriptures is best viewed as a corollary process in which God, through the presence of His Spirit, "breathes" their meaning into human hearts and creates new life.

[8] Several SBC leaders have echoed the words of Richard Land, director of the SBC's Ethics and Religious Liberty Commission, during the debate on the *BFM2000* at the Orlando SBC meeting. Land said, "All of us believe in the lordship of Jesus Christ. But we believe the only Jesus Christ we can know is the Jesus Christ revealed in Scripture. I fully believe that a demonic spirit could come and sit on the foot of my bed tonight and say, 'Richard, I am Jesus. I want to tell you everybody is going to heaven and you don't have to worry about it anymore.' But that would be wrong. . . . Why? Because Scripture stands in judgment of my experience, not my experience in judgment of Scripture."

105

Dr. Land's analogy does more than demonize those who disagree with his interpretations of the Bible; it flirts with the unpardonable sin. No Baptist that I know has ever had a vision of a demonic Jesus saying everyone is going to heaven. I do know some women whom I believe the Spirit of God has called to serve as senior pastors. To insinuate that those who believe God calls women to serve as pastors are listening to a "demonic spirit" is to risk speaking against the Holy Spirit. "Whoever shall speak against the Holy Spirit, it shall not be forgiven him, either in this age, or in the age to come" (Matt 12:32).

[9] John 19:7.

[10] 2 Corinthians 3:2-18.

[11] Galatians 3:13.

[12] Cf. Paul Ricoeur, "The Logic of Jesus, the Logic of God," *Christianity & Crisis* (24 December 1979): 324-27.

[13] John 16:13.

UNSHACKLE THE SERVANTS OF GOD

BY CATHERINE B. ALLEN

"Do not be afraid." The biography of Jesus starts and ends with these words. They were spoken to women. Women still cling to these words today.

"Do not be afraid," said God's angel to Mary. "With God all things are possibl.e" (Luke 1:30, 37)

"Do not be afraid," said God's angel to women who ministered with Jesus. "I know you are looking for Jesus. He has risen. Come, see, go, tell." (Matt 28:5-7)

"Do not be afraid!" The risen Jesus Himself said it to the women. And he added, "Go. Tell."

FEARFUL WARNING FOR WOMEN

Except for Christianity, no world religion or "ism" has ever offered women freedom from fear. Global consultations on evangelization of women in 1992 and 1993, sponsored by the Women's Department of the Baptist World Alliance, reported the following insights that many find alarming but not surprising. Most world religions blame women for whatever goes wrong. Most religions keep women at a distance from their essential promises and truths. Women have all the burdens of maintaining the faith in their homes, but none of the benefits—unless the men of their families and communities decide to pass on some of their own benefits. As a result, women live in fear. They fear displeasing men at home and in the religious community. Only by pleasing men and preserving their families do they have any hope in this life or eternity in the other world religions.

The situation of women in Christ is a beautiful contrast that Jesus offers to women—a "perfect love that casts out fear" (1 John 4:18). Paul wrote that "God has not given us a spirit of fear, but of power, and love, and self-control" (2 Tim 1:7).

Christianity is the best deal on earth or in heaven for women, although the Southern Baptist Convention's 1998 and 2000 revisions of the *Baptist Faith and Message* have obscured that truth, as this chapter later discusses. Women have everything to gain in Jesus. Through the missionary era of the last two centuries, strategies to minister to women have proved highly effective at the cutting edges of missions.

This is why the more recent *Baptist Faith and Message* statements are a tragedy for women and a disaster for missions. Without the full message of equality of males and females under God in Christ, the Christian faith becomes just another religion that empowers men to trample women. And it's not just a female problem. Doctrines of male superiority place unjust burdens upon men that God never intended.

Since the International Mission Board and North American Mission Board imposed the 2000 *Baptist Faith and Message* (*BFM2000*) as a mandate on all Southern Baptist missionaries beginning in 2002, consequences for missions will be enormous. How can missionaries, male or female, be effective when they themselves fear loss of appointments and when they have lost freedom of conscience? Christians who seek to live under the mind of Christ and the compassion of Christ must recognize *BFM2000* as self-destructive to the Baptist cause and harmful to people around the world.

THE DOCTRINE OF WOMEN

The most novel and deadly additions in the *BFM2000* deal with women. Missions has been the arena where Southern Baptist women had two centuries of utmost opportunity to serve. Women have done a world of good in crossing cultural barriers to plant the gospel and ministry of Jesus Christ in hearts and homes of women. This chapter attempts to show some practical problems in missions created by *BFM2000*.

What about Jesus?

Women who are hobbled by the new *Baptist Faith and Message* find themselves in the good company of Jesus Christ. The new doctrine also hedges Jesus. According to the new doctrinaire attitude, Jesus is subordinate to the Bible as translated and selectively interpreted by *BFM2000* writers. Perhaps the most substantive change was the deletion of key phrases found in the previous edition:

The criterion by which the Bible is to be interpreted is Jesus Christ.

… the sole authority for faith and practice among Baptists is Jesus Christ whose will is revealed in the Holy Scriptures.[1]

Many doctrinal points hinge on these statements that may be addressed in other chapters in this book. They are also pivotal to women and to missions.

All the major world religions have documents that they consider sacred. Christians have the Bible. But people in other world religions have no reason to believe that the Bible is superior to their preferred holy writings.

The exceptional appeal of Christianity is the chance to relate to Jesus Christ, the living Person and Presence. No other world religion has such a figure. People who convert from non-Christian cultures usually come via the attractiveness of Jesus Christ. They may hear of him from accounts based on the Bible, but they follow Jesus out of personal connection, not because the Bible tells them to.

Such people sometimes discover Jesus through supernatural revelation. The *Baptist Faith and Message* leaves little room for a mystical approach to faith. Some Southern Baptists, who actually engage in work among least-evangelized peoples, are praying that Jesus will supernaturally speak to the non-believers. The power of the Holy Spirit in the human heart is the only way that billions will open their minds to the Bible, God's inspired written word.

The ever-tightening noose of the *Baptist Faith and Message* demands that converts first pledge allegiance to the Bible and deny any extra-Biblical impressions they think they experienced with Jesus. Only then can their confession of faith be accepted.

Women and Jesus

Those who have searched the Bible for any gender-specific rules are particularly sensitive to the Jesus issue. "Filter everything through Jesus," advised Dorothy E. Sample, president of the Southern Baptist Woman's Missionary Union, 1981–1986, when women's issues were becoming especially controversial in the denomination.[2] This principle of biblical interpretation brings balance to the few references in the New Testament that some construe to limit women. If Jesus is not the criterion for Bible interpretation, Christianity loses much of its appeal.

Jesus has magnetic appeal for women around the world. W. O. Carver, the first academic teacher of missions among Southern Baptists and a progressive on women in missions, noted that the most significant social statement in the Gospels was "Now Jesus loved Martha." Carver said that no other central figure of a world religion could be said to love a woman without destroying his mission. "Without discrimination, woman's place in the ongoing of the gospel has the sanction of Jesus," Carver taught.[3]

Among the women students whom Carver taught, approximately twenty-nine percent became missionaries. Many male missionaries appointed prior to the 1950s also sat at his feet. They staked their lives and ministries on a firm belief that the gospel is for women without any "ifs, ands, or buts." The need of women was always at the forefront of Southern Baptist Foreign Mission Board (FMB) policy as long as Carver's teachings were honored. Carver has more recently fallen from the favor of the SBC spokesmen theologians.

Who Will Reach and Preach to Women?

The "new frontier" of missions during the last decade was "unreached people groups." Most mission boards gave careful attention to large blocks of population that do not have enough Christian believers to sustain a self-propagating church. The current Southern Baptist International Mission Board (IMB) also reassigned personnel from institutional approaches into church-starting among least-reached people groups.

They did so, however, seemingly without giving strategic attention to the specific requirements of reaching women and meeting their desperate human needs. The historic idea was that organized, trained, and informed indigenous women church leaders would quickly mobilize to take the gospel to other peoples. This was true as Baptist women in Nigeria, Kenya, Korea, Japan, the Philippines, Brazil, and Mexico started and sustained appointment of missionaries from their own people. Women in some of these countries have managed to continue impressive ministries without IMB participation; others have struggled. The IMB is not likely to encourage such a women's strategy in nearly 100 countries where the IMB claims to work, but where there is now no viable organized network of Baptist women.

BFM2000 restrictions on women merely ratified what the IMB (and also the North American Mission Board [NAMB]) had been doing as policy for several years. This policy ignores the chief characteristic of unreached people groups — that the women of those groups suffer degradation, humiliation, and severe restriction. The only way to reach women behind veils and walls and illiteracy is for other women to enter their world carrying the Good News of Jesus.

BFM2000 makes it unlikely that women missionaries in the mold of such legendary missionaries as Lottie Moon and Bertha Smith will come forward in service or be able to preach and counsel with power and authority among men. The most precious heritage of women missionaries in the past—those who crept successfully into the cultures of China, Nigeria, and Brazil—cannot be continued in Afghanistan, Iraq, or Northwest India, where women's needs are acute.

Separate and Unequal

Glendon McCullough was chief executive of the Southern Baptist Brotherhood Commission, a now-abolished agency for mobilizing men and boys in missions. He had begun his ministry as an employee of Woman's Missionary Union. In a speech in the 1970s, McCullough reminded WMU that the world could never come to Jesus, unless every woman accepted responsibility equally with men. "We can't do the job if half the potential workers are benched," he said.

That's exactly what *BFM2000* does to women. It benches them. It puts them in a separate category of potential workers. It bars them from doing many things that God might command.

BFM2000 now specifically limits women from the "office of pastor." Through two hundred years of missionaries from North America, Baptist women often served in pastoral leadership roles, even if custom prevented them from formalities accompanying the role. In fact, IMB records indicate that some ordained women ministers have been found in the missionary ranks since the 1920s. Several have been full-charge pastors of churches. Among the present missionary force, a few women are ordained for pastoral work, but have been told not to practice it. Around the world among Baptists connected with the SBC through missions, women pastors are not uncommon. In fact, they are essential.

The "office of pastor" is barely mentioned in the New Testament and is not defined. Now, contemporary Southern Baptists are faced with ambiguous definitions of what sorts of "pastoral" roles women may actually perform in churches. Among those in question in some quarters are the jobs of chaplain, counselor, teacher, director of Christian education, minister of music, minister to children.

The Doctrine of Family

Perhaps the strangest and most revealing pitfalls in the *Baptist Faith and Message* may be found in a lengthy commentary on the "Family" article in the version adopted 1998. The article itself was printed on one-half page of the 1998 *Annual of the Southern Baptist Convention*. The interpretive commentary adopted along with it covered three full pages (78-81).

According to the *Baptist Faith and Message* revisers, the husband assumes responsibility "for his wife's spiritual, emotional, and physical needs." The husband must "humble himself" to care for his wife's dominating "need for love and nurture." The husband is exclusively accorded "headship," which reflects God, and is responsible for leadership in the family ("servant leadership," that is).

Women are assigned the role of "helpers." "Leadership patterns in the family are consistently reflected in the church, as well," according to the edict. Women's acceptance of their subordinate role must be done "graciously" and "joyfully."

Within this framework, women are at last given a ministry role in the Kingdom of God. "This humble and voluntary yielding of a wife to her husband's leadership becomes a resource for evangelism, an opportunity for glorifying God, a channel for spiritual growth as ultimately the wife trusts herself to the Lord, and a means of bringing honor to His Word." In other words, the wife can trust God only after she yields everything to her husband. She becomes an evangelist only as she demonstrates the joy of being totally dominated by a husband, as by God.

111

Anybody who wants to live according to the *Baptist Faith and Message* should first consider who does much of the work in Baptist churches. What would happen if women quit taking leadership or initiative or responsibility? What would happen if they stopped contributing funds?

Worldwide, two-thirds or more of lay Christian workers are women. They serve as elders, deacons, prayer meeting leaders, Bible teachers, youth leaders, women's group leaders, ushers, decorators, visitors, and janitors. The exemplary church growth in Korea, and other places where cell groups have been organized, depends mostly upon women. The survival and expansion of churches in China were in the hands of simple laywomen.

With church membership predominantly female in most places, and with many women in church without participation of a husband, why would the *Baptist Faith and Message* insist that only men be the leaders in church?

Cultural Complexity

If the masses of Southern Baptists ever read this complicated, contradictory mixture of pretty words in the 1998 commentary on the "Family," most would laugh. In fact, passage of the Family amendment to the *Baptist Faith and Message* got headlines and laughs on every continent. The ideas seem rooted in a "never-never land" of 1950s American suburbia. The husband is commanded to "provide" for his family and the wife is commanded to "manage the household and nurture the next generation." These gender models are not biblical and are not workable in most countries of the world.

Women produce eighty percent of the food supply of Africa. Most women in certain ethnic groups of Africa engage in commerce. All this work is typically done with babies strapped on their backs. What would happen if the women retreated inside their households and waited for men to "provide"?

Couples are often seen together wading in the rice paddies of Asia. What if women stopped their economic function in that continent?

Statistics show that the ratio of widows to widowers is about four to one worldwide. More than fifty percent of elderly women are not married. More than thirty percent of women over age forty-five in Africa, Asia, and the Pacific are widows. What if these women had no experience in "providing" for themselves and their families?

One can only sympathize with the backbreaking labors of women with short hoes in the agricultural fields of Eastern Europe. But does God really want them to quit feeding their families?

Women and children do handcrafts to earn the cash income of many families in Southeast Asia. Their low wages and harsh working conditions seem criminal to Americans. Should we condemn them for going into the marketplace? Or should we shoulder our own responsibility for global export-import laws that force them to work at slave wages?

Women have been required to enter the workforce in totalitarian countries. They had no choice. They are fortunate if they are able to place their children in day care centers. Husbands and wives and children have been forcibly separated by work requirements. Do such circumstances mean that couples are not living according to Christian precepts?

In the Muslim Middle East, a man provides for his wives and family, all sharing equally in poverty or perhaps oil wealth. There, women are often forbidden to work in the public sector, cannot drive, cannot be first class citizens in their faith, and are restricted to nurture of children up to age seven. *BFM2000* sounds alarmingly close to that mind-set.

It might be great if men around the world could and would find ways to provide economically for their families. But why does the *Baptist Faith and Message* excuse males from the important command to "nurture the next generation"?

The point is that no sensible, feeling missionary would think of preaching against the ingenious struggle of men and women to survive. Their survival tactics are not a matter of faith or doctrine, but of practical necessity.

These cultural questions would not enter into the discussion of doctrine or missions, except that the International Mission Board now demands that missionaries promise to "carry out responsibilities in accordance with and not contrary to the *Baptist Faith and Message* statement," as noted in IMB President Jerry Rankin's letter to missionaries urging them to sign an affirmation of *BFM2000*.

HOW WOMEN STRENGTHENED MISSIONS

From 1845, missions was the glue that made Southern Baptists stick together. Baptists believed that even women were sacred souls who also had to confess Jesus Christ as Lord and Savior personally. That meant missions! Missions reached out to women hidden in the crannies of culture, as well as to men in the public square.

The other missions taproot was the devoted labors of a million women and girls who considered missions as their special high calling. Actually, SBC missions floundered weakly until women came forward in public leadership of the gospel. That began to happen in 1872, when the Foreign Mission Board first appointed women as full missionaries in their own right. At the same time, women's mission societies began to be organized in local churches, with grudging endorsement of the SBC.

The next hundred years were a golden century for missions, with the Woman's Missionary Union providing the fuel. Two-thirds of the missionary force were women, who crashed the culture barriers for their own sake and for the sake of the gospel. They planted the gospel firmly in the homes of China, Nigeria, Brazil, Mexico, Japan, and a hundred other countries. With the women came innovative ministries other than that of ordained pastors—such as schools, health care, literacy, and social work.

Then, in the late 1970s, the SBC got really scared of women. The trail of tears about women's roles in the SBC has been partially documented in other writings.[4] It could not be coincidental that the conservative crackdown of 1979 came just a few months after the denominational missions agencies (and others) held a public consultation, which affirmed new roles for women in ministry.[5]

It is no wonder that organizers of the Cooperative Baptist Fellowship (CBF) in 1991 listed the women's issue as one of six characteristic distinctions that distanced them from the SBC.[6] CBF has become a model of the egalitarian treatment of women.

Restrictions on women are a point of pride with the new fundamentalist leaders of the SBC. The Southern Baptist Conservatives of Alabama in Spring 2002 posted on their web site a chart by Daniel Akin, Academic Vice-President and Dean of Theology at Southern Baptist Theological Seminary. He presented the women's issue as one of nine contrasts between SBC factions. He noted that "Theological Conservatives . . . oppose women as pastor" and labels women "complementarians in the home/church." He noted that "Theological Moderates . . . affirm women as pastors" and labels women "egalitarians in home/church."

What About Women Missionaries?

No matter how often the SBC has laid down the law to women, women have just kept on becoming pastors, deacons, corporate executives, and biblical scholars, but fewer of them did so as Southern Baptists.[7] What many women *did not* become in the 1990s were missionaries. At least they did not choose missions to the extent that women did in a previous generation. This seemed to be exactly the objective of the "conservative resurgence" leaders. In 1993, the truth came to light. Former SBC President Adrian Rogers, one of the hyperconservative chiefs, revealed his objectives in an informal, but well publicized conference with key Foreign Mission Board staff members.[8] (The Foreign Mission Board is now renamed International Mission Board.)

Rogers said that the Woman's Missionary Union must be "hard-wired" into the control of the Southern Baptist Convention, forsaking their 105 years as an autonomous auxiliary to the SBC. Rogers made it clear that WMU would lose its role in SBC decision-making unless it submitted to SBC control. He wanted WMU to be kicked off its voting positions on the SBC Executive Committee, the Inter-Agency Council, and the Missions Education Council.

He further said that he regretted the "feminization" of missions. He said that missions promotion in churches should be led by pastors and by men, not by the WMU. One missions leader in the conference reported that Rogers saw WMU in an "ominous light." Rogers stated that missions needed a "more masculine look."

What Rogers wanted, he got. A reorganization of the SBC ensued in 1995, with WMU reduced to footnote status, stripped of its initiatives to organize missions education and fund-raising.[9] What followed were the rewrites of the *Baptist Faith and Message* statement in 1998 and 2000. Thus, Rogers and his colleagues showed that they were willing to sacrifice the cause of missions in order to whip women back into the silence of the early 1800s. Such capers led Keith Parks, the deposed president of the Foreign Mission Board, to conclude: "The SBC no longer finds its core and cohesion around missions."[10]

Truth and Consequences

The truth about women in missions in the SBC comes when missionaries believe, practice, and teach an inferior status for Christian women. Such doctrine is sweeping away the very foundations of missions in the SBC. For example:

- Missions promotion in the SBC has been removed from the loving arms of laywomen and placed into the hands of male clergy and denominational bureaucrats. Abused and debunked, women are slipping away from their voluntary labors for missions. WMU enrollment declined nearly thirty percent in a decade. The *Baptist Faith and Message* statement now prohibits the kind of leadership WMU has exercised.
- The big frontier of unmet missions need hovers over women and girls without Christ. Yet, if Southern Baptist missionaries believe that men are worth more to God and to SBC strategy than women, they may give only marginal attention the eternal souls of women.
- The undone tasks of missions require increased numbers of career-oriented missionaries, and the majority of them should be women. Women, after all, are still the majority of church members. Only women can witness and minister among women of some cultures. But the work that women missionaries once did as Baptists has already begun to be squelched under present doctrinal understandings of the SBC.
- Women hold the greatest reservoir of financial resources for future missions expansion.
- Human needs ministries will diminish in SBC missions. This shift in policy ignores (or perhaps not) the fact that the primary human sufferers are women and children. The shift away from social ministries is obvious at the North American Mission Board. It cut back staff (including a key woman) in September 2000.[11] Other major staff members of NAMB resigned from leading Christian social ministries in protest of anti-woman policies.[12]

Already social ministries have taken a major hit. Albert Mohler, president of Southern Baptist Theological Seminary, would not work with the woman who was dean of the Carver School of Church Social Work. From the beginning of his office at SBTS in 1993, he demanded that all faculty oppose women in ordained ministry. When Dean Diana Garland presented a faculty candidate who refused to limit women in ministry, Mohler fired Garland as dean. Ultimately Mohler declared that social work was "not congruent" with the purposes of theological education and sold off the school of social work. Thus, a foremost denominational spokesman sent the message that future missionaries and church staff need not be trained for social work.[13] This shift from an eighty-year-old strategy would remove many job postings that women (and many men) traditionally preferred. (Incidentally, Mohler's wife was one of the framers of the 1998 family revision to the *Baptist Faith and Message* that lived on in *BFM2000*.)

• The rise and fall of missions in other denominations indicates that if women are not fully affirmed in Southern Baptist missions work, it will fail. SBC missions seem therefore doomed to decline.

THE CHRISTIAN MESSAGE FOR MALES AND FEMALES

BFM2000 sets aside the weightier matters of Jesus Christ (Matt 23:24-25), and thus deserves the rebuke of Christ and Christians. The principles of God's grace always make males and females individually and equally responsible before God in matters of spirit and of daily life. *BFM2000* distorts a few exceptional passages to lay down gender-specific roles in family, church, and missions.

The central truth of the Christian faith is that "we must all stand before the judgment seat" (Rom 14:11-12). "The Son of Man will come in the glory of his father with his angels and then reward each according to his or her works" (Matt 16:27). No amount of rules about gender roles can set aside the necessity for each person to hear, repent, believe, confess, and give an account to God. No woman can hide behind a man.

Why Have Gender Doctrines?

Making gender a matter of doctrine never occurred to Baptists, including Southern Baptists, until 1997–1998. The article on "Family" added by vote in 1998 was unprecedented in major Baptist "confessions" or "statements" of faith.

For 400 years Baptists have been somewhat guided by various doctrinal statements. Not one of the major statements of faith used by Southern Baptists ever found it necessary to mention gender issues.[14]

Confessions written by Baptists in the USA did not even address marriage as a doctrinal matter. Some statements devised by Baptists in Europe and Latin America did mention monogamous marriage as a doctrine. Not a single statement prescribed unique roles limited to men or to women.

Southern Baptists prospered with a generalized minimalist application of doctrinal guidelines. The Baptist way of personal connection to God through Jesus Christ boosted many believers over the barriers of custom, culture, and language. Local conditions and natural characteristics may have segregated women and men into particular roles at times. But Baptists kept their faith statements open to the fresh winds of the Holy Spirit.

Then came the 1998 revision of the *Baptist Faith and Message*, the first major Baptist confession of faith ever to define unique roles for each spouse in marriage. It placed wives under the "servant leadership" of their husbands. Next came the 2000 revision, restricting women from pastoral roles in the church.

The framers of the 2000 statement, chaired by Adrian Rogers, stated that ". . . we have been charged to address the 'certain needs' of our own generation. In an age increasingly hostile to Christian truth, our challenge is to express the truth. . . ." The committee also stated that the article on "The Family" was added in 1998 to address "cultural confusion with the clear teachings of Scripture."[15] To this observer and many others, this subtle statement reached for a lost era when many Southern Baptist women stayed home to raise large families in rural and suburban churches, giving the churches an unlimited supply of free labor for ministries under the authority of the male pastor.

The 1963 *Baptist Faith and Message* statement might not have been approved, except that a preamble was added to assure Baptists that "Such statements have never been regarded as complete, infallible statements of faith, nor as official creeds carrying mandatory authority."[16] That phrase got lost in *BFM2000*, as Southern Baptist conservatives in the United States grasped for cultural social security.

While the later revisions to the *Baptist Faith and Message* dealt progressively with the racial revolution that emerged after 1963, it back-pedaled on women to a place where Baptists had never been before.

DO SOUTHERN BAPTISTS HAVE A CREED?

My pastor for many years at Mountain Brook Baptist Church, Birmingham, Alabama, was Dotson M. Nelson Jr. He was a denominational statesman of the old school, president of Alabama Baptists, member of the SBC Executive Committee, and competent scholar of the Greek New Testament.

The 1963 *Baptist Faith and Message* was structured by a widely representative group of Southern Baptists. It was aired in the press and before leadership groups before coming to the convention as a whole for approval. When the SBC Executive Committee discussed it, Nelson voted against it, and he was proud of his vote. Nelson went to his grave warning that the *Baptist Faith and Message* would become an enforced creed. He correctly foresaw the day when the statement would be manhandled and mandated. He made another prediction that could yet come true: that correspondence and personnel records of missionaries would be opened for public doctrinal scrutiny and purging.[17]

Creed phobia again erupted when the 2000 statement was hastily presented for adoption at a Southern Baptist Convention. As in the draft of the 1998 amendment, group members were not selected by virtue of office, but by favoritism of the SBC president. Their reports came just before vote time, without time for widespread study and response.

Nevertheless, each was adopted over the vehement protests of several spokespersons who attempted to amend or defeat the drive to get it approved.

In 2000, the vote was taken by a show of hands, with no recorded vote count. News reports estimated that the negative vote was slight. Fewer than forty percent of potential registered voters were female. The representation of females in the audience was by no means proportional to females in church membership (estimated to be fifty-seven percent in a late 1980s survey). At best, no more than 0.05 percent of Southern Baptists actually had a chance to vote on the statement.

Yet the denominational machinery immediately began to enforce the statement as a creed mandated for and by all Southern Baptists. "Believe it or leave it" was the apparent motto of SBC administrators. True, the statement can have no direct force on a person or a local church. But corporations controlled directly by the Southern Baptist Convention can demand that their employees adhere or move on.

In 2002, expansion of the *BFM2000* mind-set led the North American Mission Board to bare its teeth toward women chaplains, taking action that NAMB staff had tried to forestall for several years. NAMB is the SBC's only authorized endorsing agency for chaplains who serve in military ranks, institutions, and businesses. It announced that it would no longer endorse women who had been ordained for ministry.

The Baptist General Convention of Texas stepped into the breach, announcing it would launch a previously planned office to endorse any called and qualified person—female or male—for the chaplaincy. The Cooperative Baptist Fellowship had already been doing so for several years.

The long arm of the *Baptist Faith and Message* stretches much farther than the national-level employees of the SBC. The pressure has been on for state conventions, associations, institutions, and local churches to adopt *BFM2000*. Churches trying to be loyal to their Southern Baptist heritage will have a hard time resisting the pressures of seminary-trained pastors, missionaries, denominational trainers, promoters, and publications, all of whom are required to agree on limited roles for women.

If a local church persists in advancing women into forbidden roles of leadership and ministry, it will lose its voice in the SBC, and likely in associational and state convention business. This has been true of my church, Mountain Brook Baptist Church in Birmingham, Alabama. This church was the leader in giving to missions among all churches in the SBC. But when it ordained women for ministry and ordained women deacons, its pastor and members lost their posts in denominational leadership.

Examples abound of churches being censured or voted out because of ordaining women. Their members will not likely be appointed as missionaries or agency employees, no matter how much money the church may contribute. In some cases, the mission boards have even rejected contributions.

But the most chilling result of *BFM2000* is what missionaries pledged to it will inflict on innocent new believers.

WHY MANY BAPTISTS FEEL BETRAYED

I write as one whose divine calling is to support missions. For nearly forty years I was devoted to promoting the Southern Baptist plans of doing missions. Never in my wildest dreams could I have imagined that the mission boards of the Southern Baptist Convention would turn against women, whose hands fed them for more than a century.

It hurts to confront the truth. Ten years passed before I could face the facts. Then in 1999 I finally read the article on family, which had been voted into the *Baptist Faith and Message* statement in 1998, together with its lengthy commentary. It was alarming, but I thought it would be ignored without direct harm the missions cause. Trusted old friends from inside the mission boards provided me information and warnings. When I put it all together, I felt a strong sense of betrayal! Still, I hoped that beloved colleagues within the IMB, NAMB, and WMU would find a way to remain true to their high calling.

Those hopes were seriously wounded in June 2000, when the SBC in session passed the revised *Baptist Faith and Message* statement. It was done with cavalier speed and callousness toward the women ministers and missionaries who would be affected.   Like millions of others, I still clung to hope for the system—for the sake of the missionaries. I could not bear the thought that my old friends in Richmond and Atlanta might actually *believe in* and *endorse* the repression of women, much less that it would eventually be taught as gospel to the unevangelized world.

Now, both the IMB and the NAMB have begun to enforce the repressive *BFM2000*. Even older missionaries, with years of faithful service under the general umbrella of the 1963 *Baptist Faith and Messsage,* are required to pledge allegiance to the 2000 edition. What will ordinary Southern Baptists in the pew do to escape this noose around the necks of women and of men who want to follow Christ? What will we do to preach a true gospel to the world?

A response begins with the individual, making sure of her or his own standing as a responsible, competent soul before God. The individual has to become a truly active Baptist, being his or her own priest. Conscious choices must be made at every hand. Different people will have different criteria. But here's what I suggest:

- Find a church that nurtures individual responsibility in spiritual matters.
- Find a church that calls every member to do his or her utmost in global witness.
- Select Bible study literature and other publications that teach truth.
- Identify with missionary-sending networks that minister to the human needs of persons, especially abused women and children.

- Screen potential missionaries and pastors and church staff members, looking for people who can think, who are free from denominational prejudice, and who really love God and people.
- Require complete honesty in reporting and accountability for money you give.
- Find mission projects that give you a voice in policy.
- Quit supporting and excusing abusers.
- Look for a new and better way to do missions.

Since the issue of women has become a dividing point among Baptists, that same issue can be used to question potential missions partners. Here are the questions I suggest asking of mission boards and any others you might consider as partners:

- Does the mission board or organization require adherence to a doctrine that confines women?
- Does the mission board major on reaching Muslim, Hindu, Buddhist, or Animist women, or others who are culturally limited in their access to the Christian message?
- Does the mission board support programs such as literacy and health care for women?
- Does the board speak out against physical abuse and confinement of women?
- Does the board require equal productivity in missions from men and women?
- Does the board give equitable pay and compensation to wives, so that they accrue pensions and other benefits in their own name?
- Does the board give support to families so that both spouses can participate in work outside the home?
- Are equal qualifications required for both men and also for women candidates for appointment?
- Are the qualifications as rigorous as you would expect for your own pastor or any other professional who serves you? If not, why would you set them loose upon unsuspecting people of the world?
- Does the board place its major emphasis on support of long-term workers who learn language and culture?
- Is the board able to retain such workers over at least fifteen years on average?

WHAT CAN WE DO?

If Southern Baptists want to share the love of Jesus with a suffering world, they have to go back to the Bible. (This is what the framers of *BFM2000* have said they want.) To do so, they must remember Scriptures like these:

We must obey God rather than men (Acts 5:29).
Why do you break the commandments of God for the sake of your traditions (Matt 15:3).
They worship me in vain. Their teachings are but rules taught by men (Matt 15:9).
Help these women who labor together with me in the Gospel (Phil 4:3).

One of the wonderful characteristics of the Bible is that it can transcend cultures and make perfect sense to all people. The task of the missionary is to present Jesus Christ and through him to teach the entire Bible truth. The truth will make people free.

Look again at Christ in contrast to the cultures of the world:

• Muslim women must cover their hair. Only their husbands can see it.
• Hindu women must swirl their *saris* over their head when bowing to idols.
• Buddhist women must never defile a monk by touching him.
• Jewish women must take care not to defile a man by sitting where he sits.

But the Bible tells us that Jesus commended a woman who washed his feet with tears and dried them with her uncovered hair. Jesus told his secrets to women. He personally taught them his highest truths. He gave them work to do—public work! He accepted their offerings and praised them. He empowered them to represent his witness to other people. He saved their lives and honor. He fed them and their children.

Will we allow a document, made by a few human hands, to take away what Jesus has given to women and the world?

NOTES

[1] The *Baptist Faith and Message* statement of 1963 can be found on several websites, on many side-by-side with the 2000 version.

[2] Catherine B. Allen, *Laborers Together with God: 22 Great Women in Baptist Life* (Birmingham: Woman's Missionary Union, 1987) 152.

[3] *Royal Service*, September 1945, quoted in "Concerns Beyond Feminism" by Catherine Allen in John N. Jonsson, *God's Glory in Missions*, privately published 1985.

[4] See chapter by Catherine B. Allen in Dana L. Robert, *Gospel Bearers, Gender Barriers: Missionary Women in the 20th Cenuty* (Maryknoll NY: Orbis Books, 2002). Also see Catherine B. Allen, *Century to Celebrate: History of Woman's Missionary Union* (Birmingham: Woman's Missionary Union, 1987).

[5] See Catherine B. Allen, "Women in Church-Related Vocations, Consultation on," *Southern Baptist Encyclopedia*, vol. 4, (Nashville: Broadman Press, 1982): 2558.

[6] Daniel Vestal, "The History of the Cooperative Baptist Fellowship," in Walter B. Shurden, *The Struggle for the Soul of the SBC* (Macon GA: Mercer University Press, 1993) 5.

[7] For a study showing the brain drain of highly qualified women from SBC ministry, see Susan M. Shaw and Tisa Lewis, "Once There Was a Camelot: Women Doctoral Graduates of The Southern Baptist Theological Seminary 1982–1992 Talk about the Seminary, the Fundamentalist Takeover, and Their Lives Since SBTS," *Review and Expositor* 95/3 (Summer 1998): 411.

[8] Robert Dilday, "Rogers says SBC should control WMU," Virginia *Religious Herald*, as printed in *Western Recorder* (9 March 1993).

[9] The SBC reorganization of 1995 was supposedly going to result in increased funds for missions. In reality, percentages of the Cooperative Program going to mission boards have declined.

[10] John Pierce, "Parks: Missions 'not Primary Agenda' of SBC Takeover Leaders," *Baptists Today* (November 2001).

[11] "NAMB cuts back social ministries, while adding evangelism positions," Associated Baptist Press (11 September 2000).

[12] Steve DeVane, "NAMB employees leave over new faith statement," Associated Baptist Press (7 August 2001).

[13] WMU had introduced the concepts of social ministry as missions through the Woman's Missionary Union Training School (founded 1907). It became the Carver School of Missions and Social Work. When the school was merged into Southern Seminary in 1963, WMU entrusted endowment funds to the seminary and deeded valuable properties to the seminary. Southern Seminary used the endowment to promote social work education within the seminary. Then in 1984 the Carver School of Church Social work was created, with Anne Davis as dean (the only woman seminary dean in the SBC). When Southern Seminary abolished the social work school, it tried to hold on to the endowment. WMU took the matter into legal arbitration and reclaimed $928,541. Part of this money went to create a new program of social work at Baylor University, led by Diana Garland. This galling episode revealed much about the new SBC attitude toward human needs ministry, toward women in ministry, and toward missions. I assisted WMU in preparing historical proofs of its claim to the endowment fund, and thus made a thorough study of the case.

[14] W. L. Lumpkin, *Baptist Confessions of Faith* (Valley Forge: Judson Press, rev. 1969; third printing 1978). Dr. Lumpkin made no summary analysis of women's issues or other matters in this book. I examined more than three dozen historic faith confessions he included in his book. I wish to thank William E. Hull, who called attention to the unprecedented nature of the *BFM* revisions concerning women, in a sermon, "Women and the Southern Baptist Convention" at Mountain Brook Baptist Church, Birmingham, Alabama (18 June 2002).

[15] *Baptist Faith and Message 2000*, Preamble.

[16] *Baptist Faith and Message 1963*, Preamble.

[17] Alma Hunt, personal friend of Dotson M. Nelson Jr., and his wife, the Rev. Grace P. Nelson, corroborated my recollection of his action.

WHY SOME MISSIONARIES WON'T SIGN A CREED

BY EARL R. MARTIN

[Ed. Note: This is the first of two chapters by veteran missionary and missions professor, Dr. Earl R. Martin, focusing on (1) why some missionaries won't sign the 2000 Baptist Faith and Message and (2) what results if they do.]

Jerry Rankin dropped a bombshell letter on the Southern Baptist Convention's foreign missionaries in January 2002 by asking them to sign a document affirming the controversial 2000 *Baptist Faith and Message (BFM2000)*. This letter from the president of the International Mission Board (IMB) did a startling about-face, reversing his previous unequivocal assurance that "As long as I am president of the IMB, no missionary will be obligated to sign a doctrinal statement" (as quoted in the *Baptist Standard*, April 8, 2002).

Apparently, subsequent denominational pressures caused him to nullify that promise. His reversal sent reverberations through Baptist mission fields and scandalized many Baptists back home. It opened the eyes of many Baptists who had naively rationalized that the political strife of two decades of takeover of the Southern Baptist Convention (SBC) by fundamentalists would somehow leave their missionaries untouched. It is a departure from Baptist history and from anything I have witnessed in forty-six years as a missionary in Africa and Europe and as a professor of missions in the United States and overseas.

Rankin began his letter by commending the missionaries for their fruitfulness and faithfulness in global outreach. He advised: "We do not want anything to deter us from moving steadfastly toward completing the unfinished task of fulfilling the Great Commission." Then he refers to *BFM2000*: "We already had in place a policy that if any missionary taught or practiced doctrinal positions in any way contrary to the *BFM* that it would be grounds for termination. Our board felt that these policies and actions provided adequate accountability to the SBC and expressed confidence and trust in our missionaries."

Rankin rationalized the need for affirmation of *BFM2000*. He said that there are some who suspect that there are missionaries who do not believe or practice as Southern Baptists should. He explains it this way:

> However, this issue [*BFM2000*] has continued to generate controversy throughout the convention and suspicion regarding some related to Southern Baptist entities that may not be in agreement with what Southern Baptists have identified as the common confession of our faith. There are many who feel strongly that those being supported by the denomination should be willing to pledge affirmation and support for the current BF&M, especially those serving with the mission boards. Failure to ask for this affirmation is creating suspicion that there are IMB personnel whose beliefs and practices are inconsistent with those represented by Southern Baptists. While we believe this is unfounded, we do not need an issue such as this to generate needless controversy, erode support and distract us from the focus on our task at such a critical time of opportunity around the world.

Rankin's request got specific: "I am asking that you sign the attached form indicating your affirmation and return it to your regional leader. You are welcome to note any area of disagreement with the 2000 BF&M."

The letter, mainly aimed at veteran missionaries, urgently pressed the missionaries to sign. By doing so, they would demonstrate solidarity in doctrinal conformity. In this way, their signatures would assure their protection from would-be detractors. Rankin justified the pressure by explaining:

> Signing this affirmation protects you from charges of heresy behind your back while you are overseas and cannot defend yourself. . . . Since all new missionaries [1,500, according to another Rankin letter] processed since June 2000, including the 1,155 new missionaries commissioned in 2001, have affirmed the 2000 BF&M, your affirmation of this revision will assure consistency in our missionary force as we serve the Lord together. This will also clearly communicate to overseas Baptists and our Great Commission partners what we believe.
>
> Just as we are expected to be financially accountable for the use of resources and morally circumspect in our life and witness, we who have chosen to serve with a denominational mission agency are expected to be doctrinally accountable to those who provide our support and send us out. There should be no reticence in our willingness to express agreement with what the SBC has adopted. Asking you to affirm the current BF&M has not been requested or required by the convention or our board of trustees, but our

board is aware of this action and does commend and support it. We are simply seeking to move beyond a continuing and potentially damaging issue that could distract us from our mission task, unnecessarily create suspicion on the part of some and erode support of you and the IMB. I cannot over emphasize how important your cooperation is in order for us to move forward in fulfilling the Great Commission.

Then widespread negative reaction overseas and at home caused Rankin to send an editorial, in defense of his letter, to Baptist state newspapers on February 14, 2002. He sought to justify the letter by giving his own brief version of the history of Baptist confessions of faith:

> Even in the 19th century, before the BF&M was written, trustees of the Foreign Mission Board required missionary candidates to affirm a doctrinal statement to assure Southern Baptists their beliefs were consistent with the generally held doctrines that distinguished the convention. Since 1970, under the leadership of [two Rankin predecessors] Dr. Baker James Cauthen, and later under Dr. Keith Parks, every Southern Baptist missionary appointed by what was then the Foreign Mission Board signed a statement that he or she had read and was in agreement with the *Baptist Faith and Message*.

Keith Parks immediately refuted Rankin's contention by circulating two letters, following up Rankin's first letter and a second letter he issued on February 19, 2002. Parks's first letter follows (as reprinted in the March–April 2002 issue of *Mainstream* journal), and he elaborates further in his "Afterword" in this book.

> International Mission Board president Jerry Rankin precipitated an agonizing choice for many missionaries with his recent letter urging them to sign the 2000 BF&M Statement.
> It means they must either give up their historic Baptist convictions that "we have no creed but the Bible" or they must give up their calling.
> Veteran missionaries who have been on the field for years "signed on" with the IMB under different requirements. They voluntarily expressed their theological beliefs, but were not forced to sign a man-made creed. Their beliefs have not changed—the rules have!
> A confession becomes a creed when others determine the beliefs one is FORCED to sign.
> It has never been clearer that the fundamentalist leaders have changed the very nature of the Southern Baptist Convention. Our charter states that the "purpose of the Southern Baptist Convention is to elicit, combine, and direct the energies of Southern Baptists for the propagation of the gospel at

home and abroad." Their [SBC leaders] highest priority is not missions. It is doctrinal conformity.

This is a determinative time for all authentic Baptists. We need the prayers of faithful Baptists everywhere to determine how we can be supportive to missionaries who represent our historic convictions.

We must not lose the very heart of the gospel and the distinctive missions commitment of our heritage. We must find a way to be true to both. The IMB no longer provides that option.

Rankin's issued a follow-up letter to the missionaries in February, 2002, acknowledging those "struggling with my request." He proceeded to delineate the background to his request:

We have been asked, "If missionaries are doctrinally sound as you say, why would they not be willing to affirm that?" . . . It is time to put this matter behind us and get on with the task of leading Southern Baptists to be on mission . . .

Rankin continued by asserting that *BFM2000* is not a creed but merely a confession of faith. In a misleading, blanket statement, he insists: "It is important that you recognize that our sending and adopting churches have adopted this confession of faith and that we agree to work in accordance with what Southern Baptists believe."

In truth, only a small fraction of the churches and membership of the SBC adopted *BFM2000*. It is well-known that actions passed by messengers at any annual convention meeting do not necessarily indicate the will of all Southern Baptists. Furthermore, actions of the convention are not supposed to be binding on the churches or on individual Baptists.

However, Rankin declared that appointed missionaries, as employees of an SBC agency, should sign an affirmation of *BFM2000*: "Just as we are expected to be financially accountable for the use of resources and morally circumspect in our life and witness, we who have chosen to serve with a denominational mission agency are expected to be doctrinally accountable to those who provide our support and send us out." *Therefore, by implication, signing the* BFM2000 *becomes a matter of the terms of employment.*

A similar circular letter of explanation came to my wife, Jane, and me as missionaries *emeriti* of the SBC Foreign Mission Board (now International Mission Board). Perhaps the reader will allow a personal observation. In many respects there is an unfortunate, distinct difference between the former FMB, under which we served for thirty-one years, and the present IMB. Such a letter would have been most improbable under the FMB.

Although it was never explicit in Jerry Rankin's communications, the request carried the veiled threat that failure to sign the affirmation would result in the missionary's termination of service. A letter from one IMB regional leader ominously cautions a missionary that refusal to sign will certainly result in direct personal accountability.

Rankin's comment about Southern Baptist "suspicions" about missionaries raises the specter of heretics or liberals entrenched within the missionary force! When Rankin wrote, "Signing this affirmation protects you from charges of heresy behind your back while you are overseas and cannot defend yourself," he was offering "protection." One missionary suggests there is irony in protection from "wanna-be" accusers. He wonders if that smacks of some kind of neighborhood protection racket! In effect, does it mean, "pay/sign or you'll be hurt"?

MISSIONARIES RESPOND

IMB missionaries have been both passively silent and actively not so silent in their response to the letter.

The Missions Review and Initiatives Committee of the Baptist General Convention of Texas in Dallas offered missionaries a confidential E-mail address to vent their feelings in strict confidence and seek assistance. At this writing, Texas Baptists had received more than 100 contacts on behalf of missionaries, including seventy-three directly from missionaries. Eighteen missionary family units had reported that they either had or would resign. Texas Baptists had approved at least five missionary units to receive transition funds, with half a dozen others in waiting.

Admittedly, that is only a small minority. But it is safe to say, based on personal observation and feedback I and colleagues have received from the mission field, that this will not be a speedy process because of the complicated logistics of disengaging families from overseas locations and a variety of other reasons. Many missionaries remain mute because of personal anxieties. Some have told friends that they prefer to resign quietly. Some have refused to sign and are waiting to see what the consequences will be. One missionary estimated that one-third of the colleagues in his region of the world had not signed at this writing.

Most of the letters come from missionaries who indicate they will not sign. A few admit that, for personal reasons, they will sign—but with great struggle of conscience. They cannot honestly affirm *BFM2000*, and yet they feel compelled to do so to maintain their ministry and/or their financial viability.

Besides my own contacts, I have read and digested letters shared by Keith Parks because of their relevance to the material in this and the following chapter. He is actively involved in the Texas Baptist initiative. For obvious reasons, I must preserve the anonymity of the missionaries who wish to remain anonymous. I will render the gist of what they have written or express their meanings through paraphrases and my own personal assertions. Otherwise, I draw upon several direct e-mail communications and certain published materials.

THE SIGNERS

A significant majority of the missionaries have by now signed their affirmation. It is interesting that International Mission Board regional leaders are asking those who first signed it during their candidacy for appointment to sign it a second time. That fits perfectly into lock-step mentality and increases the IMB's ability to report a high percentage of signers.

For Some, It's "No Problem"

Beyond the 1,500 new missionary appointees that Rankin says have signed since June 2000, there are many others who have signed it because they fully agree with it. That's their right. However, there is no telling how many people signed despite their misgivings about the content of *BFM2000*. For them, it was simply a matter of the terms of employment.

For Others, It's "A Big Problem"

Critics of signing *BFM2000* point out that the real issue is not how many sign or do not sign. The real issue is that they should never have been put in that position in the first place. They argue, as *Baptists Today* editor John Pierce points out in another chapter in this book, that "in the light of Baptist history and diversity, room should be left for the individual priesthood of the believer, despite the numbers involved."

The IMB placed administration of signing in the hands of its regional leaders around the world. The onus was put upon them to enforce conformity. The intensity of persuasion has varied according to each particular region. Nevertheless, Rankin's letter implies that each regional leader bears the responsibility for 100 percent compliance. Consequently, many missionaries may feel the need to sign reluctantly because of pressure from their leaders and their peers.

For many, the requirement to sign presents serious dilemmas of different varieties. There is clear indication that many may have to sign after wrestling with the issues of what it means for their calling, their ministries, and their financial future.

Rankin's letter introduces a severe predicament for individuals. In some areas, it becomes a catch-22 among colleagues. For veteran missionaries it is more of a problem than for the younger missionary generation, although some younger ones have also balked at signing. The dilemma arises either from the idea of signing a creed or from differences with the specific content of *BFM2000*.

The letter induces anxiety among many missionaries about possible termination of their service with the IMB. Some couples are nearing retirement age. If they resign prematurely or are dismissed from missionary service, they forfeit their well-deserved retirement benefits. For some, resignation or dismissal means the loss of ministry and removal from the endearing people among whom they have served. Leon Johnson, missionary to

Mozambique, succinctly states: "For some, this is a crisis of faith in which they feel God calling them to sacrifice their conscience for their ministries" (E-mail to Earl Martin, April 18, 2002). For many, it is a combination of anxiety over financial security and concern over loss of ministry among a people they love.

Some missionaries express in interviews and E-mails a keen sense of insult over the IMB trustees' notion that some missionaries are doctrinally unsound. It would be more scriptural for any questionable convictions on the part of missionaries to be dealt with on a one-on-one basis, rather than on the blanket signing of a creed. Let those who raise such issues step forward and dialogue directly with the "suspects"!

Other missionaries express consternation that their track record as veteran missionaries, previously approved, should be called into question after years of faithful service.

Rankin's letter also presents a crisis of conscience. Let me suggest several different scenarios. The missionary signs but has to be untruthful to do so. He or she may not honestly agree with all of the *BFM2000* revisions. It makes one an authentic hypocrite to sign and not carry out his or her ministries in accordance with the document.

On the other hand, one might sign, not accepting, and still carry out the required responsibilities in full accordance. Or else, the crunch comes when one signs, giving points of disagreement, and then is forced to implement the *BFM2000*, contrary to his or her points of disagreement.

For example, let us suppose that a missionary serves in a culture where there are already women serving as pastors. By signing the *BFM2000*, the missionary agrees to the stipulation that only men may be pastors, even though it may be contrary to his personal convictions and even though it might not fit the culture in which he lives and works. His signature means that he should fulfill his responsibility and actively work toward the removal of women pastors. He faces the immediate challenge of personal integrity—to honor one's responsibility or one's convictions.

Clearly for the IMB leadership to impose such dilemmas on missionary personnel is conscionably questionable. In an open letter to Rankin and the trustees of the IMB, published by many different Baptist sources, William R. (Bill) O'Brien, former FMB missionary and executive vice president, had this to say:

> An elected administrator of a mission agency is certainly accountable to those who elect him or her. But mission administrators and trustees also ought to be the strongest advocates for the missionaries and adversaries of anything that will distract them from effective service. It now appears the [IMB's] administration has become an advocate for a denominational system that puts them in an adversarial role with the missionaries. There may be a denial of this charge.

But whatever the intended outcome of this request to our missionaries, the consequences are horrendous.

THE NON-SIGNERS

Many missionaries face a painful quandary: to sign or not to sign? to sign or to resign? to sign or to be fired? The courageous few who refuse to sign constitute a significant minority. They have engaged in the same intensive struggle with the dilemma as those who have signed. The non-signers have been able to resist the external pressures and to overcome their own personal anxieties in declining the invitation to sign. They have spurned the call for conformity to a human document that they consider to contain error.

Missionary Leon Johnson contends, "A few of us have come to the point where we have to take a stand" (E-mail to Earl Martin, April 18, 2002). Stan Lee, missionary to Rwanda, where we once served together as colleagues, has made public his refusal to sign in a letter. He expresses his unequivocal stand with the words, "I cannot do that [sign the affirmation] and remain true to God and His word" (E-mail to Earl Martin, April 15, 2002).

Missionaries Give Various Reasons Not to Sign

Missionaries who won't sign *BFM2000* give various reasons, including (1) it is a creed; (2) it is political; (3) it contains unacceptable elements; (4) it requires carrying out *BFM2000*, even if one disagrees with portions of it; and (5) it is fallible and violates Jesus Christ's prohibition against taking oaths.

(1) It is a creed. In his original letter, Rankin wrote: "I am asking that you sign the attached form indicating your affirmation . . ." Later, in a meeting with state Baptist editors, he defended the letter by strongly denying "that Southern Baptist missionaries are being forced to sign a creed in order to continue to serve . . ." He said, "We're not imposing a creed on anyone . . . Our missionaries should be doctrinally accountable to those that send them out . . ." With what amounts to doublespeak, he claimed, "We're just asking them to affirm what they already affirm." Notwithstanding Rankin's disclaimer, most of the anonymous missionary respondents to Texas Baptists, along with others who are willing to be known, insist that they are being asked to sign a creed.

It is the request to sign the document that in effect makes it a creed! This is an important insight. In response to Rankin's letter, Leon Johnson asserts that he will not sign. He defends his refusal by articulating the difference between a confession of faith and a creed: "Now, if I make the statement, 'The BFM is a faithful representation of my personal beliefs,' I am making a confession of faith. I am affirming the accuracy of the description of my faith in the BFM." Johnson continues:

However, if I affirm or sign a statement to the effect that, "I agree with the BFM," I am affirming a creed. The content of the BFM sets the boundaries of belief. It is prescribing what beliefs must be adhered to by me. It functions in this case as a creed. I may express agreement or disagreement with the BFM as a way of stating whether or not it accurately describes my beliefs. However, if I affirm or sign a statement that I agree with it, I am stating that my beliefs conform to it and it therefore acts as a creed.

This may seem subtle, but it is extremely important that we understand exactly what we are doing. Small, apparently innocent compromises may lead to the erosion of fundamental principles. The difference in wording may seem insignificant, yet ultimately, the authority of the Bible is at stake.

If a descriptive statement of belief is freely given, it is a confession of faith. The statement in no way prescribes what one must believe.

If, however, I am compelled to make even a descriptive statement of belief, it becomes a creed. In other words, if I am required to make the state-ment, "The BFM is a faithful representation of my personal beliefs," I am affirming a creed. The element of compulsion transforms the confession of faith into a creed because it is now prescriptive. My beliefs are being defined by the "confession" I affirm. It is impossible to require anyone to affirm a specific confession of belief. It is no longer a confession of faith if one is required to affirm it. (Leon Johnson, "My Response to Jerry Rankin's 'Request,'"February 15, 2002; selected from his collection of E-mail messages titled "The *Baptist Faith and Message* Signing Saga," to Earl Martin, April 18, 2002.)

Keith Parks contends that the requirement to sign *BFM2000* signifies a serious devia-tion from biblical material and from historic Baptist principles. It insults the faith of missionaries. There's a blanket of suspicion hovering overhead. In a published letter, Parks comments, "This demand for a creed is heresy in itself, from the standpoint of the Bible, as well as Baptist heritage. It is demeaning to missionaries who have already stated and demonstrated their doctrinal acceptability." For those who fail to sign, the unfair presump-tion will be that, regardless of the real reasons, they are not doctrinally sound.

Stan Lee's letter has been widely circulated through many Baptist news sources and by E-mail. It is remarkable for its clear and bold resistance to the idea of signing a creed. Lee asserts, "I do not believe any organization or church or government has the right to try to induce me to sign a pledge of affirmation to any man-made document. My allegiance is to God's Holy Word and that alone. . . . But to pledge to any other document outside God's Holy Word violates my beliefs as a Baptist and my integrity before God."

Lee wonders if the IMB leadership may think he is too audacious in his refusal. He draws an analogy from the award-winning movie *Chariots of Fire.*

Now it may be that . . . this sounds impertinent of me, a lowly veterinarian with no seminary degree, but I am reminded of one of my favorite scenes in one of my most favorite movies, "Chariots of Fire." Eric Liddell has learned that the qualifying heat for the 100-yard dash is to be held on Sunday, and he has informed the representative of the British Athletics Committee that he would not be able to participate due to his belief that the Lord's Day must be set apart as Holy. In response, the committee "invites" him to meet with them and the Prince of Wales to see if they can find a way to "help" him compromise his beliefs and run the race that he is scheduled to win as they could not go "hat in hand to the frogs" and ask them to shift the heat for them. The Prince of Wales smiles and explains to Eric, "A matter of national pride you understand, Liddell." Eric replies that he thought it was an impractical solution and that he had intended to confirm with the representative that he would not be able to participate "even before you called me in to this inquisition of yours." One of the older lords in the meeting is angered by this response and says to him, "Don't be impertinent, young man!" Eric, in a rare flash of righteous indignation, replies, "The impertinence, Sir, lies with those who seek to influence a man to deny his beliefs!"

Lee concludes, "I suppose that would be my response to those who seek to 'encourage' me to sign a pledge of allegiance to the *Baptist Faith and Message*." (Letter of Stan Lee to Jon Sapp, regional director for the Eastern Africa Region International Mission Board of the Southern Baptist Convention, February 23, 2002.)

(2) It is political. Some missionaries deplore the request to sign because they see it as a *political power play*. It is perceived as an extension of the takeover politics that have dominated the SBC for over twenty years. Denominational politics have intruded into the missionary arena. It is enlightening to read several letters and messages that reflect dismay at the obvious ploy behind the signing requirement. Leon Johnson says:

I'm hoping that this issue will not create divisions among our folks on the field. I have a suspicion that it may be part of the reason behind this. The whole BFM change/signing thing appears more and more to me as a political strategy to divide Baptists and get rid of those who won't bow down to a power hungry group who want to impose their own will on everyone. Hope I'm wrong. (E-mail to Earl Martin, April 18, 2002)

Larry and Sarah Ballew, IMB missionaries to Macao, East Asia, for six years, wrote the following words to their adopting congregation, Blacksburg Baptist Church in Blacksburg, Virginia. The purpose of their letter was to elicit prayer support for the anxious times ahead.

> . . . Sarah and I have communicated to our leadership that we will not sign the requested document. Our Regional Leader told us that at the time no decision had been made regarding the consequences of our refusal to sign. The implication in what is being said is that our termination is a very likely result.
>
> We do not want to be fired. We do not want to participate in the political power struggles of the SBC. We do not want to be used as pawns in the game either. But we cannot sign this creedalistic statement.

Rankin concluded his letter to missionaries by asking missionaries to respond to this statement: "I have read and am in agreement with the current *Baptist Faith and Message*." It then asks them to check either a "Yes" or "No" box.

This manner of responding is cast in terms of black and white. Even though the missionary who checks "No" is invited to state his or her differences, it will not matter in the final report of signers vs. non-signers. Several missionaries believe that the invitation to state differences is merely a stratagem to appear to be fair. They believe what the IMB really wants to know and to report is "Who signed?" and "Who didn't sign?" They believe that it's highly unlikely that any of the IMB staff in Richmond, Virginia, or any of the trustees will bother to read the stated differences.

Leon Johnson, who had anticipated the IMB's action, commented on the idea of it even before Rankin's letter was distributed. He posed a well-known but pertinent analogy about responding to a "yes" or "no" question:

> I am reminded of the story of a lawyer who wanted to discredit the character of a witness on the stand. He demanded a "Yes" or "No" answer to the following question: "Have you stopped beating your wife yet?" The man had NEVER beaten his wife. If he responded "Yes," the lawyer would tell the jury: "You see, he admits that he was once a wife beater." If the man responded "No," the lawyer would tell the jury: "You see, he's still a wife beater."
>
> Those who may seek to cause trouble will likely claim that failure to sign an affirmation of the *Baptist Faith and Message* is an indication of faulty faith and practice. They will fail to or refuse to understand the basis of the historical Baptist resistance to creeds. (E-mail from Leon and Kathy Johnson to Diane Randolph, October 15, 2001)

Missionaries see through what many feel is a subterfuge and clearly understand the political ramifications of Rankin's request to sign. Many believe that the overriding concern is control. An obedient missionary force is the order of the day. In his well-publicized email, Stan Lee makes an insightful allusion to Nebuchadnezzar and the "image of gold" in Daniel 3. Whether or not one agrees with Lee's application of Nebuchadnezzar's decree to the IMB's requirement to sign *BFM2000*, it is important to acknowledge that it is how he perceives it. It is my impression from all the correspondence I have seen that Lee is not alone among the missionaries in his perception that the motive to control lies behind the signing issue.

(3) It contains unacceptable elements. Some IMB missionaries—especially the veterans—demonstrate full awareness of the issues pertaining to revisions in *BFM2000*.

Expressed concerns of missionaries parallel three of the "Troubling Factors" that Russell Dilday first stated in his widely circulated document, *An Analysis of the Baptist Faith and Message 2000*, that he has adapted into a chapter in this book. These concerns follow Dilday's factor #1, the deletion of the christocentric criterion for interpretation of Scripture; factor #7, the narrow interpretation of the role of women in marriage; and factor #8, the narrow interpretation of the role of women in the church.

Christocentric response: There is ample evidence that many missionaries disagree with the removal of Jesus Christ from the *BFM* statement as the criterion for biblical interpretation. Their center in Christ is non-negotiable. The dynamic of their calling demands obedience to him as Lord as they interpret the Bible in the context of a host culture. They know full well that Jesus Christ is trans-cultural. They know full well that Jesus Christ is the indispensable ground for presenting the gospel and for interpreting the Bible to the people of the world.

Role of women in marriage: Many missionary couples have practiced mutual submission in marriage throughout their careers. *BFM2000* emphasizes unilateral submission of the wife. For these missionaries, the biblical precept of mutual submission is the natural Christian mode of the marital relationship. The enlightened missionary model of a mutually consenting relationship can be a powerful testimony in any host culture. That applies to the USA as well as overseas. Therefore, the one-way submission of wife to husband decreed in the *BFM2000* is quite unacceptable.

Role of women in church: Many IMB missionaries serve in cultures where women are as equally acceptable as men to serve as pastors. It is certainly true in matriarchal societies. It is also the case in other cultures as Christian believers experience the enlightening word of Scripture that in Christ there is *neither male nor female* and realize that the Bible cites specific examples of women in ministry. The prescribed exclusion of women from serving as pastors becomes a sticking point. So does the inevitable expansion of that prohibition to prevent women from serving in other roles of leadership.

However, there is a consideration that may affect the attitude of missionaries. When couples are appointed as missionaries, both are commissioned. It is also the case with single women. The act of commissioning may be considered the equivalent of ordination. There is a legitimate sense in which missionary women may be considered ordained ministers of Christ. Therefore, when *BFM2000* reads, "the office of pastor is limited to men," some missionaries intuitively sense that it is wrong to exclude women from any leadership role in ministry. The rationale is that since missionary women are accepted as commissioned ministers of religion, likewise, women should be accepted as pastors.

(4) It requires the carrying out *BFM2000*, even if one differs with it. One veteran couple's decision to resign from the IMB hinges primarily on this concern: signing means they must perform their ministries in keeping with all of the content of *BFM2000*. Rankin's letter offers the opportunity to sign by noting differences. However, upon signing, even with differences noted, the missionary is obliged to carry out mission work in full accord with the content of the document. The couple states that their loyalty to the Bible precludes acceptance of a document that in their understanding is not in full accord with God's word. Therefore, they cannot in good faith carry out their service accordingly.

(5) It is fallible and it violates the prohibition against oaths. Missionaries Larry and Sarah Ballew cite two more reasons for not signing that are distinct from the usual points given above. For one they suggest, "This document, by it's own admission, is fallible. . . . this is a human document"(Blacksburg [VA] Baptist Church website).

A second point they make is this: Signing such a doctrinal creed is contrary to Jesus' injunction against oaths. They point out: "Jesus instructs us to take/make no oaths. This document is asking us to violate an instruction of Jesus Christ. Our yes is yes, and our no is no. We have for years said yes to Jesus. In 1996 this yes was affirmed by the IMB. We expect them to stay true to their word as we have stayed true to ours. Nothing else is needed to be true to Christ."

THE CONSEQUENCES OF NOT SIGNING

Jerry Rankin, in an earlier statement to a group of Baptist state editors in Albuquerque, New Mexico, on February 12, 2002, commented that "it hasn't been decided whether international missionaries that refuse his request to affirm the 2000 *Baptist Faith and Message* will be asked to resign." Rankin said some have presumed that missionaries who refuse his request would be fired. He called that "pure speculation." Non-signers who don't resign but leave it to the "powers that be" to decide on their termination are in a kind of limbo.

Some IMB regional leaders had indicated that the final decisions would not be made until sometime in late 2002. The waiting becomes a form of emotional torture. The painful suspense brings an ominous sense of certain abandonment. It enhances the anxiety of situations that are already fraught with frustration. The agony will become increasingly intolerable. One missionary cries out, "Save us the anguish."

Those who resign have saved themselves the uncertainty about service with the IMB. Nevertheless, uncertainty remains with regard to how they will be able to fulfill their divine calling to missions. Texas Baptists have taken a serious initiative to render transition assistance to missionaries who leave IMB service over matters of conscience. A number of other Baptists in the Mainstream Baptist Network in several states followed the Texas lead to help with temporary transition funds, many deciding to funnel their funds through Texas Baptists, who said they would help missionaries from any state.

As of this writing, Texas had received about $1.3 million from inside and outside the state for transition assistance. Some missionaries take encouragement in the fact that Keith Parks, now retired as both president of the IMB and global missions coordinator for the Cooperative Baptist Fellowship, serves on the missions review and initiatives committee of the Baptist General Convention of Texas. Some express hope that alternative sending agencies will provide new opportunities for former IMB personnel at some point.

We have taken a careful look into the issues arising from Jerry Rankin's controversial letter. Its adverse impact on missionaries is enormous. The question remains, *What is its impact on the peoples among whom the missionaries serve?* The next chapter considers its repercussions for the signers, for missionary relationships, and on the host peoples and cultures where the missionaries serve.

WHAT HAPPENS WHEN MISSIONARIES SIGN?

BY EARL R. MARTIN

A MATTER OF CONSCIENCE: WHAT HAPPENS TO THE SIGNER?

The previous chapter explored the *crisis of conscience* caused by Jerry Rankin's request that Southern Baptist missionaries sign the 2000 version of the *Baptist Faith and Message* (*BFM2000*). Now, let's look more closely into the minds and hearts of those who signed *BFM2000*.

Admittedly, many signed it with no qualms. They either agreed with it easily or rationalized it by saying to themselves, "It's only a piece of paper." However, those who merely acquiesced to sign, without fully accepting the document, may well face the pangs of conscience. They must deal with the personal question of whether or not one is guilty of self-deception and/or hypocrisy. Former missionary to Bulgaria, Paul Ridgway, suggests: "They [IMB missionaries] are also encumbered by the guilt factor imposed by Rankin when he insists that he 'is sure that the missionaries will remain true to their call'" (E-mail to Earl Martin, April 23, 2002).

Conscientious missionaries would find it painful to fail to carry out the full expectation of Rankin's request—"In accountability to the International Mission Board and Southern Baptists, I agree to carry out my responsibilities in accordance with and not contrary to the current *Baptist Faith and Message*." The ordeal of deciding whether or not to sign has placed a burden on those who signed, but only did so with serious reservations. It makes them highly reticent to talk about it with their colleagues. Missionary Stan Lee of Rwanda, East Africa, relates his experiences with fellow missionaries:

> No one knows anyone's response unless they tell you. It has been my observation that those who have signed generally do not enter into discussions about the matter. Those who do not want to sign tend to be more vocal and if someone who has not signed talks to someone who did sign, the one who has signed

tends to remain very quite and tries to divert . . . [the] conversation to other things. I have met no one who is vocally supportive of signing this affirmation, outside of the [field] administration. (E-mail to Earl Martin, April 15, 2002)

COUNSEL FOR CONCERNED BAPTISTS: DON'T PREJUDGE THE SIGNERS

Various passages in this and the previous chapter laud the brave stand of non-signing missionaries. But the readers must never see them as reflecting judgmentally on missionaries who did sign. Their reasons are private. Therefore, Baptists inclined to agree with the non-signers and to cheer their courage should remain compassionate and sensitive to the many signers who faced a thorny dilemma. Most have agonized over the choices and have resolved their decision according to their perception of the better option. To respectfully give them the benefit of the doubt is better than to criticize. We must not wish their ongoing career to be burdened with guilt. In the spirit of Jesus Christ, they deserve our prayer support as much as do the non-signers.

The turmoil overseas is troubling. The IMB has created an exceedingly lamentable state of affairs. Does its stance send a message that doctrinal purity is more important than the stability and fruitfulness of cross-cultural missions? Out of his region in Africa, missionary Leon Johnson articulates the confusing alternatives:

> I've encouraged some friends to sign if they could without feeling guilty. Their ministries are too important to sacrifice because a group of ambitious people create problems. Others I've encouraged to join us in refusing, if their convictions are really strong. I'm personally convinced that God can be asking each of us to sacrifice something different. For some of us the price may be losing the life we love serving in our countries. For some it may mean sacrificing deeply held convictions in order to continue to provide a witness where it is needed. My only lack of compassion is for those in administration who try to get us to sign, with our fingers crossed if necessary . . . (E-mail to Earl Martin, April 18, 2002)

Johnson's words aptly illustrate the frustration and ambivalence that have prevailed in the missionary decision-making process.

A MATTER OF FELLOWSHIP: WHAT HAPPENS BETWEEN SIGNER AND NON-SIGNER?

The fundamentalist mind-set is innately divisive. The contention that continues between the current Southern Baptist leadership and dissenting Southern Baptists, who deplore the prevailing creedalism, has made a great impact on the missionary force. It has poisoned interpersonal relations of many missionary colleagues.

A Rift Among the Missionaries

The evils of strife and alienation have spread contagiously from the controlling leaders of the SBC to the cadres of missionaries around the world. In an open letter to Jerry Rankin, president of the International Mission Board, former missionary and mission board executive vice president William R. (Bill) O'Brien makes this complaint:

> The seeds of division are now planted. Suspicion of each other's position on signing may lie hidden in the depths of the missionaries' hearts until Satan seizes the moment to bring the bud to full blossom. The witness of a would-be harmonious mission family will have been blunted by the Evil One's sowing discord on one side of the ocean in America and then guaranteeing a way for it to spread to every continent—all on the wings of a pious articulation of doctrinal soundness.

When some—the minority—won't sign, while others—the majority—have signed, it readily becomes a matter of troubled peer relationships. It usually plays out in alienation between veteran missionaries and the more recent appointees. Missionaries find it necessary to be selective. Gary Baldridge, Co-coordinator of Global Missions for the Cooperative Baptist Fellowship (CBF), relates an experience from his previous service with the IMB. It illustrates the strained relations disrupting the fellowship of current IMB missionaries:

> Once in ex-Soviet Central Asia, I was working with some fellow Southern Baptist missionaries when someone broached the subject of the Old Testament problem of war. One very conservative missionary cited a passage about God's order to kill the women and children. When I commented about it in a way that gave a less [rigid] view, he did a double take and replied: "Why, I can quote you chapter and verse!" Others were present, and I suddenly realized that I would either have to become more guarded in what I said or would need to start looking for another organization through which to fulfill my calling. (E-mail to Robert O'Brien, April 12, 2002)

A MATTER OF CROSS-CULTURAL SENSITIVITY: WHAT HAPPENS IN THE HOST CULTURE?

There's a regrettable Southern Baptist ethos that too often informs the conduct of IMB missions. It operates out of a unilateral, we-know-what's-best-for-you attitude. Often, when a new missionary moves into a host culture, he or she bears an underlying air of cultural superiority. It can become an arrogant Southern Baptist/USA-to-the-world way of doing missions—or it can mature into a sensitive understanding of how to bring Jesus Christ, not American Southern Baptist culture, to a foreign land.

Cultural Sensibility: An Imperative

Missions is an endeavor that should evolve into a partnership. Certainly, in areas where missions work is established, a national body of Baptist churches already exists. Partnership becomes the ideal. On the other hand, in an area of pioneer missions, partnership waits for the development of maturing churches. An African Baptist leader, who chooses to remain anonymous, explains it well: "Partnership in mission has both horizontal and vertical dimensions. Partnership with God and partnership with one another. God is the initiator and the primary agent of mission."

The African leader continues by affirming what such partnership means, especially for African Baptists:

> The church in Africa is seriously developing a theology that is authentically African. In 1988, All Africa Baptist Fellowship met in Durban, South Africa, to address the theme, "Partnership in Mission." We met with our mission partners. We came out with the Durban Resolution. Resolution # 9 states:
>
> "As we address ourselves to the work of mission in Africa, we need to pursue our efforts holistically and in partnership with each other. In a spirit of fellowship, mutual respect, shared responsibility, interdependence, respect for human dignity, integrity, self-government, and self-expression, we need to face the challenges of our continent. Why is it that whilst there are so many Christians and churches in Africa, our continent is so poor and weak and our people suffer so much? What difference are we as Baptists making in Africa?
>
> "We call upon Baptists in Africa to dedicate themselves to the work of mission and discipleship. We commit ourselves to planting and discipling churches; developing authentic male and female African leadership; developing equipped local and national churches which can effect personal, social and economic empowerment and begin to care effectively for our environment."

My wife, Jane, and I began our missionary service in 1956. We went to East Africa as members of the founding team of seven missionary couples to begin Southern Baptist work in Kenya and Tanganyika (now Tanzania). It was a pioneer work. Before our arrival, no Baptist churches by that name existed in the two countries. Our clear purpose was to share the gospel of Jesus Christ with Africans and to establish Baptist churches.

In learning the Swahili language and the culture of the region, we understood that polygamy was a continuing practice. It was particularly evident in rural areas. It poses a dilemma when a polygamist professes faith in Christ and seeks baptism. Do you require the man to put away all but one wife? What happens to those he renounces? Should they be consigned to social isolation, poverty and/or prostitution? That happens in a culture pre-conditioned to that lifestyle.

Our missionary team came to a unanimous conclusion about how to approach the potential problems. We decided to faithfully teach the biblical principles of Christian marriage and to encourage the African Christians to deal with the matter in their churches as the problems arose. It may be admitted that one possible reason for our *laissez-faire* approach was to avoid having to settle such thorny problems. However, it was also because we clearly sensed that it would be wrong for us, as outsiders, to dictate an ethical standard on our African Christian hosts.

We did not agree with polygamy as a Christian lifestyle, and we could teach that, but we could not expect Africans to move abruptly from one approach to another until they had the opportunity to find more lasting solutions by applying their Christian faith in harmony with their own cultural norms. It is the way of honoring our freedom in Christ rather than applying doctrine quickly and harshly.

Africans dealt with this in several ways—including the African polygamist who decided to live with only one wife—his first wife. But he continued to provide for the other women he had married, and their children, because his Christian convictions would not allow him to evict them into a culture that would label them as outcasts and force them toward prostitution to survive. Missionaries who have applied teaching on marriage abruptly and thoughtlessly have created pain and devastation they never anticipated.

Likewise, when we went as the first Southern Baptist missionaries in Rwanda in 1977, Jane and I were committed to serve in close collaboration with the Baptist Union of Rwanda and its churches. We soon realized that union churches practiced policies that did not always match our customs. For one thing, financially strapped churches charged new converts a baptismal fee. Even though I did not agree with the practice, I determined not to involve myself in their denominational politics. I could express myself, but that concern was not a high priority in a country that needed the undiluted message of Jesus Christ as Savior and Lord. Baptismal fees were a matter of local church autonomy.

141

In Europe, while serving as founding director of the Institute for Missions and Evangelism at Ruschlikon, Switzerland, I faced another challenge. In the theological environment of European Baptists, I learned to deal with a rather significant doctrinal difference that pertains to standard Southern Baptist dogma. The traditional Southern Baptist stance with regard to the finality of a believer's salvation is expressed sometimes in the phrase, *once saved—always saved.* It is also spoken of as "the eternal security of the believer." It may be found in Article V of *BFM2000.* However, the majority of Baptists in Europe, east or west, hold to the contrary doctrine described by the words, *to fall from grace.* It means a believer may "unbelieve" and become lost again. In my teaching of evangelism, it became clear to me that I had to make room for a healthy discussion of both points of view. My respect for the seasoned faith of Baptists in Europe required that I make appropriate allowance for their beliefs to be freely aired. I could not force my understanding on them.

My point is this: Out of my own experiences and the experiences of others, I learned an important lesson. Missionaries must have an attitude of deference toward national Christians, their faith, their ways of doing evangelism, and their ways of doing church. Efficiency and quick results are not the best criteria in overseas ministries.

Of course, it is imperative to maintain the essentials of the gospel of Jesus Christ and the time-honored principles of Baptist heritage. But it's not vital that Baptists in Africa, Europe, or any of the continents do and believe all things strictly as Southern Baptist Americans do and believe them. Not even all American Southern Baptists can agree among themselves!

Exporting *BFM2000* into global arenas violates a sound missionary approach that shows appropriate deference to the host cultures. The point is reinforced by Eleazar Ziherambere, who has served Baptists in Africa commendably in many ways. Eleazar and I were co-pastors in founding the Baptist Church in Kigali, the capital of Rwanda. He writes:

> What I am saying here is the tendency of some Mission agencies to exhibit an attitude suggesting that they are the sole ones who can hear God's language and therefore, being the sole ones who know the heart of God. This way, they send men and women called "missionaries" to go to propagate their own views about God. Such attitude presupposes that they are the only ones who have the message of God. On the field, one may be amazed to discover that God can speak not only in English but also in Swahili, Yoruba, Zulu, etc. . . . [missionaries need] to hear together with the Nationals what God is telling them to do for the people there in their own context rather than bringing our own context from America to impose it to the people on the so called "mission field." Instead of giving a set of creeds to travel with, we should allow our missionaries to travel with God and with the people they are to serve, to encourage them to listen carefully [to] the voice of God and do whatever he tells them to do. (E-mail to Earl Martin, April 21, 2002)

One thing is certain. Overseas Baptists do not want the dictates of *BFM2000* imposed on their churches. Regardless of professed good intentions to the contrary, that's what is happening now. The truth is that Baptists around the world want none of it. Bulgarian Baptist, Theo Angelov, general secretary of the European Baptist Federation (EBF), expressed his concern:

> Our position is that we don't want the controversy in the U. S. over the BF&M, as well as all the other points of controversy, to be imposed in Europe. We have enough problems to deal with! We know some missionaries who have been affected by this, but we don't want to interfere in a battle which is not bringing good results. . . . The EBF is developing a good mission work, especially in Eastern Europe, and we are happy that until now in our European Baptist family we have [had] a good spirit of unity. I hope that we will continue in this same way in the years to come. (E-mail to Earl Martin, April 24, 2002)

Is it even possible that the intentions of the SBC with the *BFM2000* could be limited only to Baptists in the US? It would be quite naive for anyone to think that such strict conformity would not worm its way into the Baptist churches and cultures where IMB missionaries serve.

The cross-cultural challenge comes when the missionary signer of a creed, such as *BFM2000*, proceeds to fulfill the responsibility that signing requires. The crux of the matter is found in the second part of the agreement form to be signed: "In accountability to the International Mission Board and Southern Baptists, I agree to carry out my responsibilities in accordance with and not contrary to the current *Baptist Faith and Message* as adopted by the Southern Baptist Convention." It is a seed of cultural imperialism. In the latter part of his first letter to missionaries, Jerry Rankin indicated that signing "will also clearly communicate to overseas Baptists and Great Commission partners what we believe."

One must ask, what may be the ramifications of the phrase "to carry out my responsibilities in accordance with and not contrary to the current *Baptist Faith and Message*"? Does it mean to teach, preach, translate, publish, and distribute *BFM2000* as a creed among people of a different culture? If it doesn't mean that, then what does it mean? Comments from Stan Lee illustrate the confusion:

> . . . there are some, many in [field] administration, who signed believing that it is something they need to do to show solidarity with the churches who have sent them to the field. However, they do NOT think that these things apply to every culture and they plan to continue to preach and teach as they have always been. One told me that in the section [of the *BFM2000*] on the church where it says that the office of the pastor is exclusively a male office, the phrase follows "as prescribed by Scripture." He takes that phrase to mean that if Scripture is

143

actually prescribing something the 2000 BFM does not, he can sign, and still teach and live in line with his own interpretation of Scripture. One of our administrators had problems with this since we have many female leaders of churches here in East Africa. He asked [a specific IMB home office administrator] if signing meant he was to teach that here in East Africa. [This administrator] told him "of course not!" [He also] told him that signing the affirmation was agreeing to this statement for churches in America but it had nothing to do with churches in Africa. (E-mail to Earl Martin, April 15, 2002)

Does the denial by [this IMB administrator] mean that missionaries are not expected to impose *BFM2000* on the national Christians? Was he, by those words, giving the official policy of the IMB administration and the trustees? Or, rather, was it his private interpretation to offer a softening of the original intent?

Notwithstanding any such disclaimer, one thing should be clear. Those who gladly signed and heartily affirm *BFM2000* will propagate it faithfully. Were the document not to exist, there are those who, because of their indoctrination before missionary appointment, are already disposed to promote its points of view. Once the missionary proceeds "to carry out my responsibilities in accordance with and not contrary to" *BFM2000*, what will it mean for national believers who disagree with it? They may disagree, either because they see it as a creed or because some of the doctrinal interpretations are unacceptable. Or they may disagree simply because missionaries are trying impose an American contrivance on them.

Once again, the aforementioned African Baptist leader aptly articulates the potential problem as it relates specifically to the signing of *BFM2000:*

> The signing of *BFM2000* of missionaries will mean that they should adhere to the doctrinal statement which will cause missionaries to use the statement as a creed. The Baptists have fought against creed throughout history. The fact is that most missionaries live with multiple identities: IMB identity, convention or union identity, local church identity and missionaries' own identity. Asking the missionary to sign the statement will result in the second question—that is, imposing Southern Baptist doctrinal statement on the local church. This imposition will result in "paternalism," that is, trying to cloth[e] the local church in the alien garment of western Christianity. Partnership in mission is a shared ministry and there should be mutual respect of partners. Paternalism is unacceptable in African Baptist community. It is an outmoded system and it has been rejected by the church in Africa.

When missionaries propagate *BFM2000* in mission areas, it creates the potential for an insidious heresy. Demanding compliance with it in the missionary situation introduces the risk of complicating the gospel of Jesus Christ. Demanding obedience to a creed from another culture creates cross-cultural pitfalls. Such conformity insinuates that all Baptists must believe alike in these matters. It's like missionaries saying, "If you would be an authentic Baptist, you must agree with this codified doctrinal statement."

It also may create cross-cultural confusion about what it means to become a true convert of Jesus Christ, as an analogous situation did in the first controversy in the apostolic church. We read about it in Acts 15 and Galatians 2. It was a major debate caused by the Judaizers, or circumcision party, that demanded the circumcision of Gentile believers before they could be accepted as full-fledged Christians. Dr. Douglas Waruta, a leading thinker and theological educator among African Baptists, articulates that analogy admirably. In a paper given at an Africa-wide Baptist theological conference, he writes:

> It is missiologically unacceptable for any Christian community to insist on reproducing itself in other cultures. That was the reason for the Jerusalem council that rejected the demands of the Jerusalem Christians that Gentile Christians embrace the Old Testament demands of circumcision as a precondition for being Christians. Of course the Jerusalem Christians were being "biblical" in their terms and the Old Testament was the only scripture they had then! Yet the Gospel of Jesus Christ refused to be guided by laws and customs and freed people to be Christians and full members of their own cultures. This is the Baptist way. African Baptists must be ready to embrace the Gospel of Jesus Christ in their own terms. This can only happen when and if they commit themselves to reading the Bible and interpreting its message for and by themselves. (Dr. Douglas Waruta, "Biblical Interpretation and African Traditional Thought," from All Africa Baptist Theological Educators' Conference on African Baptist Theology and Identity [Ibadan, Nigeria: Oritamefa Baptist Church, November 8-10, 2000], 50.)

Interpersonal Relationships Between Missionaries and Nationals

The furor over *BFM2000* has not only inflicted wounds on the fellowship among missionaries. It also has had an adverse effect on the host cultures where missionaries serve. When that happens, what does it say to national believers? Does it tarnish the witness of missionaries? Does it diminish confidence in their ministries? Will such divisiveness become contagious and infect the life of the national churches? These are crucial questions to consider.

Professor Alexandre Castro, of Baptist Theological Seminary of South Brazil, wrote to Richard and Carolyn Goodman Plampin, retired SBC missionaries to Brazil. In his message he relates the following incident: "It is nearly unbelievable, but in a meeting of the faculty of the seminary, a fundamentalist American, in a moment of fury against what I said, even laid the doctrinal statement of the [Southern Baptist] Convention on me. . . ." (Alexandre Castro, in an E-mail, April 10, 2002 with the subject: "Fundamentalism/Calvinism in

Brazil"; translated from Portuguese by Carolyn Goodman Plampin in an email from Plampin, April 11, 2002.)

Recently retired missionary Paul Ridgway predicts:

> About BF&M, the IMB has already stated that their missionaries are going to propagate BF&M. This is going to cause disagreement and distrust and controversy with Baptist unions (national Baptist denominations). It is going to build walls around the IMB and make them more isolated than they already are from local Baptist churches and unions. When problems arise in points of doctrine, the missionaries will be forced to adhere to the "letter of the law" and not be understanding of or open to points of difference in interpretation. (E-mail to Earl Martin, April 23, 2002)

Ridgway continues his email by giving a perspective from his service with the IMB in Europe. He asserts:

> There is also a sense of "spiritual superiority" that results from this (*BFM2000*), as already seen in the SBC for a number of years. This is quite dangerous and could lead to the missionaries establishing separate churches which will not cooperate with local unions. Either the churches will be dependent on the missionaries or will wither and die without some aspect of cooperation. How can we as Baptists preach adherence to a man-made document [*BFM2000*] rather than to the written Word of God? It is simply incomprehensible what IMB is asking the missionaries to do! Realistically, however, the missionaries in Europe are not having much impact on starting churches. Local unions (national Baptist denominations) are having much greater success at this, with or without the IMB's help. Seen from the eyes of local union leadership, I believe that missionaries who sign the BF&M are going to lose a degree of credibility, but the ultimate question is whether their ministry and witness will be able go on in the light of the adherence to denominationalism instead of to the person of the Lord Jesus Christ. (E-mail to Earl Martin, April 23, 2002)

For some missionaries, the major stumbling block posed by *BFM2000* involves the role of women in ministry. This is true throughout all of the continents where IMB missionaries serve. In some areas, it is a case of the cultural role of women in matriarchal societies. In other cultures, where Taliban-like men cruelly suppress women, they need an undiluted view of the love and freedom of Jesus Christ. In other areas, there is a new awareness of the implications of biblical material that overrules the distinction between male and female leadership.

Five quotations, three from missionaries and two from national Baptists, express concerns:

From an African Baptist leader:

> On women in ministry—The SBC operate[s] under the assumption that women should not be ordained for ministry or become church leaders. This assumption is being challenged from many quarters within the Baptist church in Africa. The church in Africa is empowering women to help complete the task of missions in Africa. It is very encouraging that significant numbers of Christian women are taking new roles of leadership in local churches and denominations. (Anonymous, E-mail to Earl Martin)

From Larry and Sara Ballew, missionaries to the East Asian nation of Macao:

> This (BF&M) is a culturally biased and culturally shaped document. It would be inappropriate for us to impose this document as a template on the work we are doing among the Chinese. To be true to this document would require us to be false to the very people we have been sent to help. We have been called out and sent forth to proclaim the Kingdom of God, not to propagate American culture. (E-mail from Robert O'Brien, "Missionaries Explain Why They Can't Sign BF&M," February 24, 2002)

From Former IMB missionary to Spain and Costa Rica, Rick Lane:

> While we were in Spain, there were two women pastoring Spanish Baptist churches. They were referred to as "missionaries" by the Spanish Baptists, but everyone knew they were pastors. Since the IMB was contributing indirectly to the support of the Spanish Home Missions work, this "awkward" situation was a constant source of conflict with the growing fundamentalist movement. (E-mail to Earl Martin, April 15, 2002)

From missionary to Japan, Lydia Barrow-Hankins:

> Women serving as deacons and pastors in Japanese Baptist churches is not a new phenomenon, nor is this church [Seinan Gakuin Baptist Church in Fukuoka City] the exception. . . . With less than 1% of the Japanese population professing faith in Jesus, the enormous need for Christian witness compared to the scarcity of Christian workers means that the Japanese church simply does not have the luxury of limiting to men the roles of deacon, pastor, and preacher of the gospel.

...When Japanese are baptized, they know they have stepped from death to life, from darkness to light, and from the assumptions and mores of their society into a new society called the Church. They have heard the gospel in the liberating, affirming attitude of Jesus that reverberates through their personal lives, relationships, and social structures. Japanese Christians, having stepped far out of certain cultural patterns, can accept women, or participate as women, as full members in the Body of Christ. ("Church Business Meeting in a Baptist Church," Lydia Barrow-Hankins, <http://www.mainstreambaptists.org/barrow-hankins.htm>)

When missionaries sign *BFM2000*, the consequences are far more serious than Rankin and the International Mission Board trustees could have imagined. We have seen its effect on many who sign reluctantly for reasons of conscience. Its power to divide has wreaked havoc on the fellowship of many missionaries.

In at least one case, the signing question has even caused a missionary couple to come into conflict. Ironically for the wife, it has to do with the matter of the wife submitting unquestioningly to her husband. Missionary Stan Lee describes their differences:

I know of one family [in East Africa] . . . where the husband and wife are divided on this issue. The reason the husband gives for signing (he has already signed) is that God called him to his place and the pettiness and spiritual sickness of these men should not be allowed to interfere with his calling. So, he signed to give them what they wanted so he can continue with his calling from God. The wife has not signed or responded in any way. Her major problem with the 2000 BFM is its view of women and marriage. She is a professional woman and to sign is, in effect, denying what she is. (E-mail to Earl Martin, April 15, 2002)

African theologian Dr. Douglas Waruta sums his reactions this way:

African Baptists, and indeed many African Christians and believers from the poor and historically deprived and dehumanized peoples of the world, have an alternative. The alternative is a Biblical and Christocentric Christianity . . . . Christocentric faith is the climax of the Biblical faith.

Jesus, through His life, death and resurrection, reveals a God who is not primarily interested in religious rituals, traditions, rigid theologies, and dead customs. For Jesus, the Torah is summarized in loving the Lord with all your strength, mind and heart and loving your fellow man as yourself (Matt 23:37-39).

Sabbath religion of legalisms, and devoid of the concern for those in need of active love, is dead religion . . . [but] the Samaritan "outcast," whose practical love for fellow human being reflects the spirit of the God of Jesus Christ, . . . puts to shame the self-righteous religion of the Pharisees and the scribes (inerrantists) (Luke 10:25-37).

When the King comes again as Judge and Lord of all, His judgment will not be based on the orthodoxy or piety of believers but on how they treated the "least of the brethren" (Matt 25:31-46). . . . For Jesus, God's people, the church, is the example of the New Humanity, the New Community of the poor in spirit. . . . [It is an example of] those who mourn, the humble, the peacemakers and those who stand in the world as light and salt, to be experienced by those around them for who they are and the difference they make in the world around them (Matt 5–7).

What Africa needs and must pursue is this Christocentric faith, for in Jesus we have God as Immanuel, with us, sharing our struggles and loving us as we are and not because we can claim special place in God's Household. God's salvation in Jesus is freely received and freely given (Matt 10:8).

What Africa needs is a Christian community characterized by a Biblical and Christocentric faith, a people after the God of the Bible and Jesus of Nazareth. The God of Manna and Mercy, not of sanctimonious theological platitudes and authoritarian traditions.

. . . we did not know that the Southern Baptists, a denomination many of us knew as committed to a Biblical and Christocentric faith, would degenerate to what has now become a tragic reality.

Some of us became Baptists because of the freedom to serve Christ and to obey the word of God without a controlling authority or godfathers. This Baptist heritage was exhilarating to many of us who had been exposed to authoritarian Christianities that specialized in controlling African Christians to become carbon copies of their own traditions and found it difficult that Africans could read and obey the word of God without reference to these founders. Baptist faith was a liberative faith based on the dignity and integrity of every Christian to respond to God's grace and love, freely.

I have read the new 2000 *Baptist Faith and Message*. I think it is a sad document for any group of Baptists. Of course, as a Baptist, I must respect those who chose to practice their faith according to the document and wish them well, for indeed there are millions who sincerely believe that it is the best way to live and confess Christ.

What is unacceptable is the attitude of some of these "Baptists" which fits very well the words of Jesus to the Pharisees: "You travel over land and sea to win a single convert, and when he becomes one, you make him twice as much a child of hell as you are" (Matt 23:15).

As Africans, we are very disappointed at the retrogressive direction some Baptists in the US have taken. Worse still, they expect the rest of the world to "learn" from them. It is about time we Africans sent missionaries to the Bible Belt [of] America! We will continue to embrace a Biblical and Christocentric faith, of our own reading, interpretation and application.

Our women will prophesy and pastor churches and if they do not, it is because they chose not to do so and not [because of a] mis-reading the scriptures to keep them from full participation in the drama of God's grace in Christ.

We will teach our wives, even against our own African traditions and customs, that in Christ there is no male or female [and that] we are all called to love and serve each other (Gal 3:28).

We will read the Bible, through the eyes of Jesus, that we have God who loves and calls men and women to come and receive the gift of eternal life, by faith and not by following a tradition or a statement of faith such as the BFM 2000.

We sympathize with SBC appointed missionaries in our midst who are made to choose between obeying their consciences and [losing] their livelihoods or [keeping] their livelihoods at the expense of their conscience. We sadly warn those SBC BFM 2000 enthusiasts to tread carefully when they come to Africa, for they might find that African Christians know Christ and will live their faith regardless of these "packaged truth bearers."

What many missionaries never learn is that Africans have an uncanny way of creatively living their own chosen faith while at the same time, in order not to antagonize their guests [missionaries], will appear to be in agreement with them! (From an E-mail to Earl Martin, April 26, 2002)

BFM2000's impact on cross-cultural missions is of particular significance. The signers, who have identified well with the nationals among whom they serve, will have a problem carrying out the demands of the document. Most missionaries know that it is wrong to impose Southern Baptist doctrine into the host cultures. They want to manifest respectful sensitivity to the beliefs of national Christians. On the other hand, the nationals are virtually unanimous in resistance to *BFM2000* or the imposition of any creedal standard. When missionaries try to convince national Baptists to adopt Southern Baptist doctrines, serious tensions emerge.

Jerry Rankin's letter has the potential to harm the lives of many missionaries. It has the potential for damaging relationships with national Baptists as well. The hurt is irrevocable. Instead of fostering solidarity, it has caused division. The impact at home is formidable.

It is time for sensible Baptists to rise up to counteract the tyranny of dogmatism in the corridors of denominational power!

AN AFTERWORD OF WARNING

BY R. KEITH PARKS

The 2000 *Baptist Faith and Message* (*BFM2000*) reveals radical changes in the Southern Baptist Convention (SBC). The convention of the year 2000 is a distant denominational cousin of the convention formed in 1845. It is still a Baptist convention. It uses the same name. But it contradicts its own heritage and violates its own constitution. The differences are many and significant:

• Suspicion has displaced trust.
• Control has displaced cooperation.
• Doctrine has displaced missions.
• Exclusion has displaced inclusion.
• Creedalism has displaced confessionalism.
• Politics has displaced fellowship.

Originally, Baptists with a great variety of beliefs came together to cooperate around the cause of missions. This is stated in the SBC Charter's Introduction to its Constitution and in the Purpose statement of that Constitution. There is no definition of doctrine anywhere in the SBC Constitution or Bylaws. I often referred to this original purpose when I was president of the SBC Foreign Mission Board (now International Mission Board).

Some "Ultra-Conservative Resurgence" leaders argued with me that doctrine, not missions, was the unifying force. It took me awhile to recognize that they were a different kind of Baptist. Some Baptists do believe doctrine is the most important element in a convention. This explains why many of them gave only minimal support to the SBC before taking control and changing its nature. They have now redefined the Southern Baptist Convention and have made doctrine its controlling force.

They may not realize nor care that, historically, groups that have formed around doctrine have split and continued to splinter.

Previously, any Southern Baptist church that wanted to support this cooperative *mission* effort was accepted on its own confession that it was Baptist. There was a trust in those who so identified themselves. Their doctrinal beliefs were not screened.

Southern Baptists brought together Baptists with varying shades of basic doctrinal beliefs for the cause of missions cooperation. Two primary historical streams of Baptists (Sandy Creek and Charlestonian Baptists) brought a wholesome tension between:

• formal worship and informal worship;
• proclamation-evangelism and ministry-evangelism;
• desire for educated clergy and suspicion that educated clergy might lose evangelistic zeal;
• thought-provoking preaching and authoritative preaching.

Like a pendulum, the struggle between these different emphases of biblical truth helped balance Southern Baptists.

The original SBC demonstrated its "Baptist-ness" by accepting a variety of interpretations. They practiced the biblical conviction that every believer has access to the Holy Spirit's interpretation of Scripture. These differences were not about basic doctrine.

Actually, the present controversy, which surfaced in the 1970s and has climaxed with *BFM2000*, is not about whether Baptists really believe the Bible. Rather, it is about whether Baptists believe the Bible in certain ways and interpret it according to the present leadership's views. It really is about control of Baptists' beliefs and actions.

The ultimate litmus test is *not*, "Do you believe the entire Bible is the inspired, God-breathed Word of God?" The litmus test *is*, "Do you believe *BFM2000*, and will you preach this interpretation and make this emphasis in your ministry?"

To those who reject this demand, convention leaders declare that the Holy Spirit would not lead the SBC Committee into error. They further declare that those rejecting it are denying the "priesthood of believers" doctrine to those who revised *BFM2000.*

This clearly implies that the select group who revised the 2000 *Baptist Faith and Message* believe they are infallible and that those refusing to sign the document are rejecting God's inerrant truth. They can certainly exercise their own priesthood of the believer, a term they failed to get deleted entirely from *BFM2000*, but they cannot reject my priesthood of the believer and expect me to sign the document.

Some leaders give another equally disturbing reason for signing *BFM2000*—that members of other denominations say they can sign every page of the Bible. For these leaders, since we all agree on the Bible, an additional criteria is required to distinguish Southern Baptists from other denominations. The need for such a distinction proves that "just believing all of the Bible is not enough to make you a Baptist."

In other words, the Bible by itself is not enough! What a frightening admission by persons who have taken over the SBC, claiming to be Baptists!

This reveals the difference between:

- creed and confession;
- trust and suspicion;
- cooperation and coercion;
- inclusion and exclusion; and
- control and equality.

The crux of the matter is, "Do I have the right under God to confess I believe the entire Bible the way Baptists generally believe it? Do I have the freedom to support the SBC and be accepted as a member in good standing?"

In the past, I could. Baptists confessed their beliefs, supported the convention, cooperated, and were welcomed into fellowship. Everyone understood there were variations of interpretations on nonessential doctrines. But there was cooperation in order to accomplish the larger purpose of missions. And there was fellowship.

That has changed. The current approach is creedal. A confession that "I am a Baptist" is no longer enough.

In a *confessional* approach, a group declares, "Here is what we believe." Others who agree with the confessional approach say, "We want to join with you in ministry and fellowship. Let's walk together."

In a *creedal* approach, the keepers of the creed declare, "Here is what we believe, and if we determine that what you believe meets our test, you may join with us."

In a confessional approach, *the one joining* makes the decision.

In a creedal approach, *the leaders* decide who may join.

The SBC constitution declares it will never exercise authority over other Baptist bodies. That has changed radically with the demands for compliance to *BFM2000*, a self-declared "instrument of doctrinal accountability."

Another misuse of *BFM2000* relates to missionaries. It is inaccurate to state that current SBC leaders are using *BFM2000* like other statements of faith. For example, a new BFM was adopted in 1963 while I was serving as a missionary. The Foreign Mission Board never asked missionaries to sign the *BFM1963* confession of faith or pledge to teach according to it.

Still another misuse of this document is the implication that it is more important than the missionaries' own expression of doctrine.

The cultural nature of *BFM2000* further complicates the situation. Current Baptist leaders have declared that our own culture has changed enough that a revision was needed.

BFM2000 is an effort to address Baptist beliefs to contemporary American cultural standards. That, in itself, acknowledges that it is uniquely American—for Southern Baptists in America. To insist that missionaries emphasize this as their standard in working in the cultures of the world contradicts good Baptist teaching and good mission strategy – not to mention good common sense.

The wonder of the God-Breathed Word is that it is "at home" in every culture. As the local people are Spirit-led, they interpret Scripture appropriately for their own culture. When one imposes one's own cultural interpretation on Scripture as the standard to be used, it can distort Scripture for those from other cultures. Current IMB President Jerry Rankin, in a letter urging all IMB missionaries to sign *BFM2000*, admitted that it "responds to an American culture that is sliding into relativism."

The IMB rationale requiring missionaries to sign is also confusing. On the one hand, some state that it that this is no different from the process they have already been through. Some IMB leaders have suggested it's merely a piece of paper and no one should have a problem signing it. Others have insisted that because there is suspicion that there are some heretical missionaries, the signing of this document would provide immunity from that suspicion.

If anyone has a specific accusation about any particular missionary, the correct procedure would be to reexamine that missionary. However, to require all missionaries to sign a doctrinal statement implies lack of confidence in their doctrinal integrity as a whole. It also belies the statement that this really is not different from what they have done in the past. Formerly, the emphasis was on the personal expression of doctrinal belief. This is much more the Baptist way than signing a statement agreeing to teach in accordance with and not in contradiction of a man-made, admittedly fallible document.

It is critical for every Baptist church and its members to make informed decisions, in light of what has happened in the Southern Baptist Convention and its institutions. Some of Baptists' finest people still serve as missionaries. Yet the direction and emphasis of the missions programs has veered sharply from past practice. Every Baptist needs to learn what those differences are.

Once one knows what is happening, a decision should be made. If one agrees with the changes, then continue support. If not, then stop or alter support. It is unfaithful stewardship to continue supporting a denominational system that one believes does not comply with Scripture or is spiritually harmful.

It is absolutely necessary for Baptists to pray and seek ways to obey Christ's command to witness what they believe is true to a lost world in a way that does not violate their deepest Baptist convictions. I join this book's publisher, editor, and chapter authors in the hope that we can reclaim the best of our Baptist heritage.

CONTRIBUTORS

Catherine B. Allen is a founder and treasurer of Global Women, Inc. She is a former president of the Women's Department of the Baptist World Alliance and a former associate executive director of Woman's Missionary Union, where she handled business affairs and specialized in researching and writing the history of WMU and of women in missions.

David R. Currie is executive director of Texas Baptist Committed and a national consultant for the Mainstream Baptist Network. He is author of numerous articles and books, including *Songs in the Desert* (Smyth & Helwys, 1999).

Charles W. Deweese is executive director-treasurer of the Baptist History and Heritage Society. He is the former assistant executive director of the Southern Baptist Historical Commission and has thirty years experience as a Baptist pastor and historian. He is the author of seven books on Baptist history.

Russell H. Dilday is a retired Distinguished Professor of Homiletics at George W. Truett Theological Seminary and special assistant to the President at Baylor University. In 2002, he was named as Interim President of Howard Payne University. He is also a former President of Southwestern Baptist Theological Seminary. Russell is the author of several books on Baptist concerns.

James M. Dunn is the president of the Baptist Joint Committee endowment. He is a retired executive director of the Baptist Joint Committee. He is Visiting Professor of Christianity and Public Policy at Wake Forest Divinity School and the author of numerous articles and books, including *Soul Freedom: Baptist Battle Cry* (with Grady C. Cothen) (Smyth & Helwys, 2000).

Earl R. Martin serves as the national prayer coordinator for the CBF Gypsy ministries team and as a missionary *emeritus* of the SBC Foreign Mission Board and the CBF. He is also a former professor of missions and world religions at both Southwestern Baptist Theological Seminary and the International Baptist Theological Seminary. He is the founding director of the Institute for Mission and Evangelism of the European Baptist Federation.

Kenneth Massey serves as pastor of First Baptist Church of Greensboro, North Carolina. He is widely involved in the leadership of national, state, associational, and local Baptist organizations. Before coming to First Baptist, he pastored churches in Texas and Mississippi.

Robert O'Brien is editor of *Mainstream*, the journal of the Mainstream Baptist Network. He also serves as writer, editor, and communications consultant for Baptist organizations. Robert has thirty-seven years of experience in Baptist journalism and ministry, including seven years as editor of Baptist Press news service and sixteen with the SBC Foreign Mission Board (now International Mission Board).

John D. Pierce is executive editor of *Baptists Today*, an autonomous, national Baptist news journal. He is also the former managing editor of *The Christian Index*, the newspaper of the Georgia Baptist Convention.

R. Keith Parks is chair of the New Initiatives Subcommittee of the Missions Review and Initiatives Committee of the Baptist General Convention of Texas. Keith retired early from the SBC Foreign Mission Board, where he served as a missionary and as FMB President. He also served as the Global Missions Coordinator for the Cooperative Baptist Fellowship.

Bruce Prescott is executive director of Mainstream Oklahoma Baptists. He is also the former chair of the Baptist Distinctives Ministry Team for the Cooperative Baptist Fellowship.

Walter B. Shurden serves as Callaway Professor of Christianity and founding executive director of the Center for Baptist Studies, Mercer University. His is also editor of *The Baptist Studies Bulletin*, a monthly E-magazine and author of numerous articles and several books on Baptist history, including *The Baptist Identity* (Smyth & Helwys, 1993).

Charles Wade is executive director of the Baptist General Convention of Texas. He is also former BGCT president, former president of the Fellowship of State Convention Presidents, and former vice president of the European Baptist Convention. He has pastored churches in Texas, Oklahoma, and Germany.